ENTERPRISE

02.04

Corporate Venturing

Nicolas King

- Fast track route to creating successful new corporate ventures

- Covers the key areas of corporate venturing from identifying the main options to setting objectives, and from aligning the interests of corporate investors and entrepreneurs to maximising your return on exit

- Examples and lessons from some of the world's most enterprising corporate ventures, including Intel, Sun, Eisai and Cambridge Technology Partners. Plus ideas from the smartest thinkers and practitioners in corporate venture investment, including Josh Lerner, Fergal Mullen, Will Schmidt and John Wall

- Includes a glossary of key concepts and a comprehensive resources guide

≫EXPRESS EXEC.COM≪
essential management thinking at your fingertips

First published 2002 by
Capstone Publishing (a Wiley company)
8 Newtec Place
Magdalen Road
Oxford OX4 1RE
United Kingdom
http://www.capstoneideas.com

CIP catalogue records for this book are available from the British Library and the US Library of Congress

ISBN 1-84112-370-6

This book is printed on acid-free paper

Substantial discounts on bulk quantities of Capstone books are available to corporations, professional associations and other organizations. Please contact Capstone for more details on +44 (0)1865 798 623 or (fax) +44 (0)1865 240 941 or (e-mail) info@wiley-capstone.co.uk

Contents

Introduction to ExpressExec

ExpressExec is 3 million words of the latest management thinking compiled into 10 modules. Each module contains 10 individual titles forming a comprehensive resource of current business practice written by leading practitioners in their field. From brand management to balanced scorecard, ExpressExec enables you to grasp the key concepts behind each subject and implement the theory immediately. Each of the 100 titles is available in print and electronic formats.

Through the ExpressExec.com Website you will discover that you can access the complete resource in a number of ways:

» printed books or e-books;
» e-content – PDF or XML (for licensed syndication) adding value to an intranet or Internet site;
» a corporate e-learning/knowledge management solution providing a cost-effective platform for developing skills and sharing knowledge within an organization;
» bespoke delivery – tailored solutions to solve your need.

Why not visit www.expressexec.com and register for free key management briefings, a monthly newsletter and interactive skills checklists. Share your ideas about ExpressExec and your thoughts about business today.

Please contact elound@wiley-capstone.co.uk for more information.

Introduction to Corporate Venturing

This chapter looks at:

» how corporate venturing competes with R&D, M&A and new business development;

» business justification – financial rates of return from corporate venturing;

» non-financial rewards – keeping in touch, loosening up the organization style;

» playing the percentages – deal flow, outperforming the specialist VCs and the stock market;

» individual careers – putting corporate venturing on the CV and the world of the in-house entrepreneur.

"Maintenance of the present business is far too big a task for the people in it to have much time for creating the new, the different business for tomorrow."

Peter Drucker[1]

THE VALUE OF CORPORATE VENTURING IN AN INCREASINGLY COMPETITIVE MARKET

In the last decade, corporate venturing has clawed its way onto the management agenda as a possible solution to the question: "How do you do better than double digit growth?" While short-term business priorities put the focus on returns to shareholders, companies have used venturing to identify the most valuable areas of growth for future performance.

Realizing the value of a corporate venture is about creating value from talent, from spin-offs, returns from an IPO, trade sale, license, tracking stock or an off-balance sheet piece of research and development. Competitive value, for example, as a way to tie-up technology so the competition can't get hold of it, or taking a stake in a possible acquisition target, is high and, as usual, counts double.

Outrageous financial returns are not impossible, though it is probably best to consider corporate venturing as an activity that pays for itself. Whatever else they might do, companies don't want to mismanage an activity that could be crucial to their survival or miss out on a class of investment, which has outperformed the stock markets for seven out of the last ten years. Corporate venturing is an increasingly important part of the tool kit for managing the risks of developing new business.

Some companies venture strategically, almost like an alternative to research and development (R&D), a way of learning about future directions in their market space and identifying companies with new products that may become important. Finding a young company or start-up that has already developed a new product can reduce development costs and time to market. Make an investment in the young company and it may deliver the benefits of innovation. An early opportunity to work with new companies can be a useful complement to a more formal acquisitions activity.

The investing company, particularly if it is large, can overcome some of the problems of size or inflexible reward structures by working with a smaller, more agile player. By structuring the relationship carefully, it can manage the risks of innovation and keep some of the costs off the balance sheet.

In the pharmaceutical industry, the venturing model is widely used as a way of sharing risks in looking for new drugs and bringing them to market ahead of the competition (see the Eisai case study). In some business cultures, venturing has become the natural way to extend the family-run business or develop a regional empire based on a network of clans. In parts of Asia, it is the customary model for extending the franchise for all sorts of retail business, from clothing to fast food.

Some corporate venturing is almost entirely about the financial returns. Finding investment opportunities in young companies with high growth potential can help meet future growth targets. Companies with excess cash to invest have set up large venture capital funds that rival the private venture capital companies in terms of their size and ambition.

In a sense, corporate venturing has grown up in the shadow of the private venture capital industry. Now, at around 15–20% of total equity risk capital, it has emerged and become established in its own right. The two work alongside each other. They participate in the same funds and invest in the same new companies.

In the past few years, around 300 companies – more than half of them in the USA – have set up programs of significant size. The only business justification for a program, of course, is if the investment delivers a better return than any alternative, over a defined period.

Over the past decade, returns from some of the large programs, where companies invest capital funds of $100mn or more, have frequently matched the performance of the private venture capital firms, which, themselves, have averaged an internal rate of return of around 15% over the past ten years. Some outstandingly managed programs have produced a return exceeding 60% a year. But the returns from corporate venturing funds are very variable and are susceptible to the peaks and troughs of the investment cycle, like everything else.

It is no accident that it has been mainly the technology companies that have set up the largest venture funds. Intel, the chip manufacturer, for example, has invested more than £3bn through its venture fund in the past three years. Over the past decade – until recently – they have been the ones with the excess cash to invest. But they are also the ones who have had to do more than anybody else to attract and retain talented individuals to fuel their growth.

A great part of the interest in venturing has come from people in technology companies insisting that they want to join the venture trail, either outside the corporation as fully fledged entrepreneurs or within it (see the Cambridge Technology Consultants case study in Chapter 7). Not simply for the rewards – normally very few qualify for participation in the funds, as opposed to the stock options, which most enjoy – but also for the taste of entrepreneurial management it offers.

Corporate venturing isn't just something that is increasingly useful to have on your curriculum vitae. The experience of working on a corporate venturing team – spotting opportunities and trying to realize their value to the company – gives you the satisfaction of being a key part of an enterprise, the sense of identifying more closely with what you do at work.

One of the people interviewed by Rosabeth Moss Kanter, the management guru and originator of the term "corporate entrepreneur," characterized this quality as "like winning a free game when you're playing pinball" – a novel but apt description of entrepreneurial management.[2]

This strong sense of identifying with the enterprise is what makes corporate venturing such a powerful tool in the business development locker. Successful venturing helps generate a corporate culture that thrives on ideas and exploiting opportunities. A well-managed program allows you to tolerate a level of risk that would normally be unacceptable, with the chance of delivering better growth than your competitors, if you exploit the opportunities successfully (see "Loosening up" in Chapter 6).

Since the Internet bubble burst, the venturing landscape looks very different from a year or two ago. Companies like Amazon and Starbuck's, which entered the corporate venture arena at the height of the Internet boom, have withdrawn their funds and cancelled their venture programs. The imperative for developing emerging online retail concepts has disappeared. Many of the media companies have also cut back their investments or withdrawn them completely.

Companies take a lead from private venture capital investors. They provide funding for ventures at a similar stage of a new business's life: towards the left-hand end of the investment path, the one that starts with seed or start-up funding, through successive rounds of development stage funding, on the way towards going public.

At the height of the Internet boom, corporate ventures along with the venture capitalists (VCs) tended to back technology start-ups at an ever-earlier stage in their development, in anticipation of gaining a proportionately larger share of the returns on flotation. They also made use of innovative financial instruments, like tracking stocks, to realize the value of their e-business subsidiaries.

Thanks to the loss of interest in technology investments since 2000, and the virtual impossibility of taking companies public, many VCs are devoting themselves to their current portfolio rather than making new investments. This means the usual leveraging effect of VC capital is missing from the investment scene, which is proving something of a constraint on corporate venture programs.

The corporate venturing function always has to justify its performance against that of the private venture capital companies, just to survive. In the past, downturns in the economic cycle brought many venturing programs to a shuddering halt and the latest wave of programs may last only as long as its predecessors, in the early 1970s and mid 1980s. Around one-third of US companies had abandoned their venturing programs as of June 2001.

Most companies just aren't as good at it as venture capitalists, which is not so surprising when their business is taking care of the shop, rather than opening a new one. They often lack the focus that VCs apply to the job and the ruthlessness that VCs show in picking up and dropping investments. Their ambitions are quite often mixed. Apple Computer, for example, obtained a strong financial return from their venture program – in excess of 90 cents on the dollar – but they rate it as a failure, because it did little to promote revenue for their core business, selling computers. The best way for corporate venturers to answer the challenge is, of course, to outperform their VC counterparts and live up to the results of the exceptional few (see "Follow the money" in Chapter 6).

NOTES

1 Drucker, Peter F. (1985) *Innovation and Entrepreneurship*, Butterworth Heinemann, Oxford.
2 Moss Kanter, Rosabeth (1983) *The Change Masters*, Thomson Publishing, London.

What is Corporate Venturing?

This chapter explains the concept of corporate venturing, including topics such as:

» where the money kicks in – the role of venturing at different stages of growth;
» realizing value – tracking stocks, IPOs, trade sales;
» cultural differences – Asian franchisers, European buccaneers;
» the big choices – DIY, outsource and hybrid corporate venturing;
» putting CV on your CV – is yours an administrative or enterprising style?;
» mini case: Iona.

"Corporate venturing provides the best of entrepreneuralism and corporate risk aversion"

Gifford Pinchot[1]

MAKING MONEY OUT OF TALENT

In its broadest sense, corporate venturing is about leveraging external resources to turn good ideas into commercial projects. Good ideas are the starting point – ideas to do with the way we work, what we consume, getting products to market faster or cheaper or better.

It is the application of knowledge – the literal meaning of technology – that turns them into profitable ventures: one of our case studies involves a business that was created literally by applying brain power to business problems (see the Parc Technologies case study in Chapter 7).

Good ideas often start off in the laboratory – an academic one or a research department of a company. But they might as well come from people chatting around the water-cooler or working in the prototyping department.

Companies with the resources in-house can work through the best ideas, sift out the promising from the non-starters and develop them into practical business applications. But many companies, due to their size or structure, can find difficulty in allocating the finance, time or resources to develop products or services in-house. Also, increasing specialization means that it is often better to leverage outside resources to commercialize a good idea.

CORPORATE VENTURE MODEL

In the classic corporate venturing model, a company spins out a new technology venture or a more established company invests its resources directly into an entrepreneurial start-up, sharing the commercial risks and rewards.

The new company is looking for the investment and expertise to promote the earnings growth it needs for a flotation or sale.

The corporate partner provides money, expertise in their industry sector and management skills. The company may make the investment all by itself or, more usually, in conjunction with venture capital companies or other investors that are also interested in the potential returns.

The venture capital partner provides equity in the new company, expertise in structuring the transaction to keep it off the balance sheet, expertise on exit to realize the maximum value; services like recruiting additional managers; and a sounding board for discussion and new ideas (see Fig. 2.1).

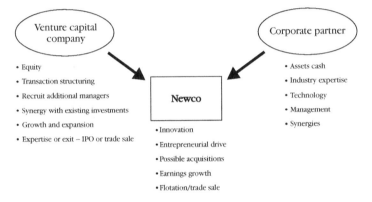

Fig. 2.1 Venture capitalist, new company and the corporate partner – what each brings to the party.

That's the model. In practice, while a corporate venturing program might be managed assiduously, every project is different. The main difference is due to the fact that corporate venturing is a people business. As long as individuals are making decisions about ventures it will have a highly idiosyncratic flavor. For example, Iona, the software company, might never have become the first Irish company to list on NASDAQ without an investment deal with Sun Microsystems struck in unusual circumstances.

Iona was unusual, in the first place, being aimed primarily at the US market. Dr Chris Horne, Annrai O'Toole and Dr Sean Baker started the software specialist company on the campus of Trinity College, Dublin, Ireland in 1993. All three of them were working as academics researching the general area of distributed object systems, with some partial funding from the European Union (EU) under the ESPRIT program. Horne and his colleagues had won a bid to work on a specification for Corba from the Object Management Group. The team spotted the potential for a software product based on Corba, and by the summer of 1993 had developed the first version of Orbix, for Windows and Unix.

They believed there was a strong demand for the product in North America, the only problem was funding its development. "Originally we each put in $1,000," says Horne. "We would have had to pay Trinity for computing services if we had carried on using their equipment, so we bought our own."

But they needed more serious investment. "We tried banks, venture capitalists and private individuals," says Horne. "But our business plan was unusual – how could you do this, in Dublin, against people such as Microsoft?"

The breakthrough came in 1993, when they launched Orbix at the OMG's Object World tradeshow in San Francisco. By chance, Sun Microsystems' stand was just 150 yards away. The team on the Sun stand immediately spotted the potential in Iona's software, for their own business. "They were quite excited," says Horne. "They came over to Dublin and asked if we could undertake a project to make our product talk to theirs, via a TCP/IP (Internet Protocol) link."

Sun had reservations. "How can we bet on you, when you're just a $100,000 company?" was the main objection. But Horne had a solution: "We suggested they buy a portion of the company."

The deal, completed on Christmas Eve 1993, gave Sun a 25% "golden share" with two seats on the Iona board, in exchange for $600,000. It meant Iona could claim Sun as a business partner, rather than a competitor. It was enough to persuade Motorola, who had wanted to use Iona but had been concerned about its financial stability, to come on board as a customer.

"They talked to Sun and, hey presto, we became their mandated supplier across their entire program for Iridium: the satellite mobile phone network," says Horne. The Irish Inward Development Authority also stepped up with matching funding, based on the jobs that Iona would create.

So long as corporate venturing is about enterprise rather than, say, investing money through a tracker fund, the weight of importance of people's judgment and entrepreneurial talent is paramount. Once companies commit to a corporate venturing activity of any size, they are saddled – or blessed – with the people that run it for them. It is the in-house venture management team that make the running, sifting out the best investment opportunities and sponsoring the program within the company.

In any entrepreneurial project, the outcome depends on many factors, but the key ingredients are the team, the opportunity and the chances of realizing its potential.

When pushed about which of these factors is the most critical to a successful investment, venture capital specialists often argue the toss between the potential of the opportunity and the team charged with realizing it. In the corporate venturing world, the team assumes a greater importance. You can change the team, of course, but while they are in place, their entrepreneurial management skills assume great significance.

CORPORATE VENTURING PROGRAMS

A feature of the past decade has been the huge corporate venture programs of the high-tech companies, like Intel, the computer chip maker and Oracle, the software giant.

This is the more sophisticated approach to corporate venturing, where a company establishes a fund to invest in start-ups or new companies either directly or through a corporate venture specialist. As the high-tech sector has boomed, companies have invested in corporate ventures as a way of getting a handle on the developments that are going to be important to them.

Corporate venture managers have had to learn to keep pace with the necessity for high growth. At one time, a company might have embarked on a project with a vague notion that it might turn out to complement its core business activity. Now, their management team adopts a more proactive approach. Some companies hardly bother to go to the auctions without having a buyer in mind for their hot new find, when they want to dispose of it (see "Exit strategy" in Chapter 6).

The size of funds under management in corporate venture programs has been catching up with the venture capital companies. Intel has invested more than $3bn over the past 3 years. In the pharmaceutical sector, the risks in bringing a major new drug to market are so high that it is rare to see one that has not been developed through a venture partnership.

In many respects, corporate venturing programs have a great deal in common with private venture capital. Companies that run their corporate venturing funds entirely for profit, rather than any strategic fit with the core business, share precisely the same issues: hands-on or hands-off investing; early stage or later stage funding; the crucial importance of the IPO market in realizing returns.

But there is an important difference for the majority of corporate venturers who are looking for strategic benefits as well as financial returns. They have to consider the triangular relationship between the interests of the parent company, those of the new offspring and the venture program managers, in the midwife role. The key issue for companies is how to organize the corporate venturing function best; whether to keep the process at arm's length or integrate it into their in-house culture; how to reward successful venture managers to stop them running off to the VC firms (see Chapter 6).

NOTE

1 Pinchot, G. (1985) *Intrapreneuring*, Harper & Row.

The Evolution of Corporate Venturing

Looking at how corporate venturing has evolved, this chapter highlights:

- » corporate venturing's landmark deal – AMD's investment in DEC;
- » milestones – peaks and troughs in a cycle of boom and bust;
- » moving in the footsteps of the venture capital specialists;
- » new technology's promise of high returns;
- » where we are today – challenges to corporate venturing;
- » the importance of enterprise culture and individual rewards.

Corporate venturing – the phrase – entered the management literature in the 1970s. There is nothing new about the concept. For decades, forward thinking companies have relied on the entrepreneurial efforts of their people to find ways of growing. It is still a young industry and daily grows more sophisticated.

Back in 1985, Gifford Pinchot, who coined the term "intrapreneur" to describe in-house entrepreneurial behavior, said: "Look back at any great business or invention, at just about any big company, and you can find that entrepreneurs created it."[1] But they missed plenty, too.

Xerox, the document image specialist, is often cited as the company that failed to exploit its own best discoveries. In the 1970s and 1980s, Xerox Parc, their Palo Alto Research Center, invented some of the best computing technology of the decade, from the GUI (the graphical user interface that Apple made famous) to the Ethernet, the high-speed local area network that links millions of PCs. But they failed to commercialize them, themselves.

Sony did better with the PlayStation computer games console – but only just. An employee, Ken Kutaragi, dreamed up the idea but when he first proposed it in the 1980s, the management team at Sony looked on a games machine as a mere toy, not a serious consumer electronics device. Kuturagi persevered and eventually his chief executive supported the project, and appointed him to lead the development team. Since its launch in 1994, PlayStation has outsold Sega and Nintendo, with sales of more than 70 million units; one in four households in the USA owns one. By 1998, the PlayStation was providing 40% of Sony's profits.

Going back even further, there used to be plenty of ways to keep people with entrepreneurial skills busy. Before the Second World War, it was common for companies to diversify, which gave plenty of scope for using entrepreneurial talent and developing more of it if required. But with the post-war trend towards big corporations, the skills that companies really needed were more to do with running a tight ship than developing in different directions. Later, the emphasis on vertical integration only served to increase focus on managing resources rather than creating new opportunities. Companies wanted to control every step of the process between production and the marketplace and this meant bringing acquisitions in-house.

So, the interest in corporate venturing in recent decades has been as much about rediscovering and recognizing existing skills as learning about new ones. Much of the interest, from a management perspective, has centered on the corporate venturers themselves. Their sometimes disruptive contribution to the enterprise has been prized or merely tolerated at different times, depending on the need to shake up the organization and promote promising new areas outside of the core business.

In the 1980s Rosabeth Moss Kanter, the management guru, recognized the contribution of people who worked in large companies but behaved like entrepreneurs. Gifford Pinchot identified the organizational issues that managers need to address to release the skills of their in-house entrepreneurs, whom he terms intrapreneurs. Since the late 1990s, the biggest names in the field, Paul Gompers and Josh Lerner of Harvard Business School have analyzed the record of corporate venturing programs and separated the cyclical factors from the management issues. This has helped put the current activity in context.

MORE RECENTLY

The main conclusion to draw about the recent history of corporate venturing is that the results are somewhat patchy. Few companies would claim to have made a great success of it. The main problem for corporate venturing is that, like the private venture capital industry, its performance suffers the cyclical problems associated with the rise and fall of the stock market. Then, on top of that, it has problems all of its own.

One persistent problem is the difficulty that companies have had in finding good talent to do the job. Even the most profitable could hardly match the rewards that an enterprising employee could expect to win outside the corporation, either by starting a new business of their own – and taking it public – or by moving jobs to a venture capital company – and sharing possibly stratospheric returns. Then again, how many employees could claim to know how to spin off a new company successfully?

How do you keep your mainstream managers happy when they can see their corporate entrepreneur peers enjoying greater freedom? How do you resolve the conflicting aims of corporate strategy and making money?

CORPORATE VENTURING PROGRAMS

Companies started setting up their own corporate venture funds in the USA in the mid-1960s, a couple of decades after the private venture capital industry, which had begun in earnest after World War II. Companies saw the success that the private venture capital specialists were having with investments, particularly in technology companies. As so often happens, one deal became a beacon. In this case, it was the monumental return that American Research & Development Corporation made on the start-up financing it provided in 1958 for computer maker Digital Equipment Corporation. By the early 1970s, almost one quarter of Fortune 500 firms had tried their hand at one kind of corporate venturing program or another.

The first programs were generally short-lived. The oil crisis of 1972 sent the stock market into decline and abruptly put an end to the prospects for new public offerings. This made it difficult for venture capitalists to realize a return on their investment and impeded their ability to raise new funds. Companies followed the VCs out of the market and curtailed their corporate venturing programs. The cyclical pattern, linked to the performance of the stock markets, was to occur over and over again.

During the late 1970s and early 1980s, the markets recovered and companies started investing in ventures once more. By 1986, companies were collectively investing around $2bn in their corporate venture programs, around 12% of total venture capital funds. The 1987 stock market crash again flattened the market for new public offerings. Returns plummeted and the venture capitalists found it difficult to raise new funds. Companies cut back on their venturing programs once more so that by 1992, the number of corporate venturing programs had fallen by one-third and the value of funds under their management fell to 5% of the total pool.

As the markets soared again in the mid-1990s, interest grew once more, in Europe as well as the USA. By 1997, corporate venture funds rose to around 30% of the venture capital pool. This time the boom continued until the end of the decade, until the stock market correction in early 2000. It was broader, too, with companies raising bigger funds, more interest outside the USA, and in firms outside the high tech sector.

TYPES OF CORPORATE VENTURING PROGRAMS

From the start, most companies have been motivated by the desire to learn more by working with other companies within their own industry sector, as well as making a profit. Those with the confidence and resources have invested directly in start-ups or new companies and managed the process themselves.

Some corporations do it ad hoc, through the finance department, the mergers and acquisitions group, the business development function, or some other business unit that happens to come up with a bright idea. Other companies create a business development group with a specified venture capital budget. Lucent Technologies New Venture Group (NVG), created as one of Lucent's business units two years ago, uses a venture capital model to develop ideas that come out of Bell Labs, the company's research activity.

Other companies have channeled their venture budgets into separate funds that aren't consolidated on the balance sheet, either making an investment in the fund's stock or in one of the funds the venture company manages. Lucent Ventures is a venture-capital arm of the company that funds ideas from outsiders, but is separate from the Lucent Technologies New Ventures Group. Other major companies with separate funds include Dow Chemical and SmithKline Beecham.

Others have outsourced the venture investment process, but retained management control, by working with an independent private venture capital specialist. Yet others have gone for a mix of all the above (see Chapter 6).

High-tech companies have dominated the corporate venturing program scene, and their fortunes – closely following the performance of the technology sector – have swung wildly. The current loss of interest in technology investments poses a wholesale threat to corporate venturing. It is leading a downturn, which also threatens to snuff out the signs of interest outside the tech sector.

Overall, periods of accelerating interest in corporate venturing normally follow strong performance of the private venture capital industry. Josh Lerner, a specialist in the field at Harvard, has conducted a review of the statistics and literature on corporate venturing and concluded that the results are not as bad as the generally poor reputation of corporate venturing would indicate.[2] In fact, Lerner concludes that far from being outright failures, corporate venture investments in entrepreneurial companies have been just as successful as those backed by private venture capital companies – particularly when there has been a strategic overlap between the interests of the parent company and the investment portfolio.

WHERE WE ARE TODAY

It is important to remember that corporate venturing is still new, especially outside of the USA. As a result, individual programs are, to some extent, vulnerable to the whim of the company treasurer – who may decide to cut it from the budget in a downturn.

Practitioners have to compete with the private venture capital companies and contend with the stock market. Many still have not demonstrated they can achieve good returns on investment over a decent stretch of time, rather than in short bursts. Until they do, company shareholders will, justifiably, question management time spent on an inherently risky activity when equal or better returns are available elsewhere.

One recent large sample study by Gompers and Lerner,[3] comparing corporate venture investments and private venture investments, found that when corporations invested in activities that were related to their own line of business, their returns actually were competitive with those of private VC funds.

The recent scaling back of corporate investment programs is a reminder of the accepted wisdom for entrepreneurs. Start-ups should not rely on a single corporate investor to provide all of its funding. They should look for strong syndicates of VCs, as well as a good combination of strategic and corporate investors.

Below is a timeline showing the milestones in the evolution of corporate venturing.

» **1950s**: Venture capital industry develops rapidly in USA and starts to develop in European and Asian financial centres.

» **1958**: American Research & Development Corporation makes monumental return on the start-up financing it provides for computer maker Digital Equipment Corporation; achieves reputed annualized rate of return of 130%.

» **1960s**: Companies start setting up their own corporate venture funds, mainly in the USA.

» **1960s and 1970s**: Technology fuels interest in enterprise; Silicon Valley and academic centers like Stanford and MIT became synonymous with new technology; venture capital firms focus investment on start-up and expanding technology companies; early successes include Intel, Apple Computer, Lotus Development and Federal Express; venture capital comes to be almost synonymous with technology finance.

» **1970s and 1980s**: Xerox Parc, the Palo Alto Research Center of Xerox Corporation, invents some of the best computing technology of the decade – from the GUI (graphical user interface that Apple made famous) to the Ethernet, the high-speed local area network that links millions of PCs – but fails to commercialize them.

» **1972/3**: Recession following oil crisis sends the stock market into decline and abruptly puts an end to the prospects for new public offerings.

» **Mid-1970s**: Almost one quarter of Fortune 500 firms have now tried their hand at corporate venturing.

» **1984**: Kohlberg, Kravis & Roberts finances the $25bn leveraged buy-out of RJR Nabisco, with debt from the junk-bond house Drexel Burnham Lambert (West Coast office headed by the infamous Michael Milken).

» **1987**: ''Wall Street'', the movie. Gordon Gecko, the callous financial buyer (Michael Douglas) takes over companies to sell off their assets, at the expense of blue-collar jobs; tells his fictional shareholders ''Greed is good.''

» **1985**: Venture Economics starts collecting the data to calculate the return on venture capital investments in the USA.

» **Late 1980s**: Collapse of communism unleashes market forces in Eastern Europe and the former Soviet Union; a rush of Western capital into the economies of Poland, Hungary, Czechoslovakia and Russia mops up some of the best investment opportunities; increased liquidity makes raising money much easier, allowing local entrepreneurs to seize new opportunities.

» **1985**: Gifford Pinchot coins the term "intrapreneur" to describe in-house entrepreneurial behavior.

» **1987**: Stock market crash again flattens the market for new public offerings.

» **Late 1980s**: Rosabeth Moss Kanter, the management guru, finds signs that high-tech companies encourage entrepreneurship among employees; carries out much of her research among large USA hi-tech companies like General Electric and Hewlett Packard.

More than 100,000 companies now use electronic data interchange.

» **1989**: Tim Berners-Lee invents the World Wide Web.

» **1990s**: Academic centers of excellence in entrepreneurship spring up; for example Babson College and the Kauffman Center, in the USA; the London Business School, UK; and INSEAD, France. In conjunction with 3i, the venture capital company, INSEAD sets up a research center in entrepreneurial management in Fontainebleau; its campus in Singapore makes it possible to do comparative studies of enterprise culture in Asia Pacific and Western markets.

» **1991**: Cisco Systems, the data networking company, launches Cisco Connection Online (CCO), a network for vendors, partners and customers.

» **1994**: Jeff Bezos founds the online bookstore, Amazon.com.

» **1995**: Michael Hagen and Michael McNulty found VerticalNet, to operate industry specific online communities.

» **1996**: Cisco adds online ordering to CCO, making it one of the first private B2B (business-to-business) exchanges.

» **1997**: GEM, Global Entrepreneurship Monitor starts; first systematic study to compare enterprise and entrepreneurial behavior between countries; collaborative project between 21 academic institutions across the world, led by Babson College, USA, and the London Business School, UK; study confirms that entrepreneurship is strongly associated with economic growth.

» **Late 1990s**: Paul Gompers and Josh Lerner of Harvard Business School analyze the record of corporate venturing programs and separate the cyclical factors like the effect of the stock markets, from the management issues, like difference in pay for corporate venture managers and private venture capitalists.

» **1999**: B2C (business-to-consumer) wobble starts. B2B seen as the real way to make money for investors, as $85bn in B2B transactions take place online

» **2000**: B2B bubble starts to pop in March.
  Hi-tech bubble bursts around May; venture capitalists retreat, dot.com marketplaces postpone IPOs.
  Big shake-out from August onwards.

» **2001**: A succession of dot.com marketplaces fail, merge or adapt to new business model.

NOTES

1 Pinchot, G. (1985) *Intrapreneuring*, Harper & Row.
2 Lerner, J. (2001) "A note on corporate venture capital", Harvard Business School, Harvard, MA.
3 Gompers, P. and Lerner, J. (2000) "The determinants of corporate venture capital success" in Randell Morck (ed.), *Concentrated Corporate Ownership*, University of Chicago Press, Chicago.

The E-Dimension

This chapter explores:

» life after the e-revolution – what the dot.com fallout tells us;
» valuing and holding on to entrepreneurial talent;
» tracking stocks;
» bricks and clicks – winners on the Web;
» mini case study – Translucis, Diageo's first e-business.

The e-business bubble marked a high-water mark in the recent economic cycle, the longest continuous period of growth in living memory. Now that the bubble has burst, it is time to pick a way through the assorted debris, to see what the tide brought in and what are the implications for corporate venturing.

In terms of investment activity, the Internet shifted the focus of funding in the second half of the 1990s dramatically towards the left-hand side of the chart, in the direction of early stage investment. Before the Internet boom, a significant proportion of risk capital went into management buy-outs (also called leveraged buy-outs), perhaps a quarter of the total in North America, but as much as two-thirds in some parts of Europe. As investors and corporates sought to cash in on the boom, up to 90% of the funding went into the riskier end of the scale.

The so-called "new economy" certainly gave expression to a powerful grass-roots appetite – as anyone who went to a First Tuesday meeting and witnessed the feeding frenzy of pitching and card-swapping among entrepreneurs and venture capitalists will testify. But not all were about to fulfil their wildest ambitions.

Developing a sustainable enterprise culture does not happen over-night. Successful enterprise is rooted in education, training, engineering and business skills. The Silicon Valley factor adds some vital ingredients, too: the comparative ease of incubating start-ups, the premises, finance, advice and buzz of the science park; above all the mass of people whose confidence in success outweighs their fear of the consequences of failure. These kinds of conditions take time to materialize and are far better developed in many places, in the USA, Canada and Israel, among others, than they are in most of Europe.

However, that did not stop many from trying, nor others from betting on their success. The traditional financing model for a growth company got well and truly squeezed. The time span from formation, through early stage funding, late stage, to an initial public offering (IPO), which had been typically 3–5 years, now collapsed towards 2–3 years. Internet time, it seemed, applied to realizing a return as well as every thing else.

BRICKS AND CLICKS

Companies embraced e-commerce in different ways. Some, like Amer-ican Express, leveraged their core business, extending the full range of its services into the e-arena. Spurred by the desire not to miss out on the IPO boom, others were tempted to run Web-based activities at arm's length, with the aim of floating and realizing value – unprecedented value.

In many cases, the corporate tail wagged the dog. The valuation of new economy stocks screamed off the right-hand top corner of the chart, leaving old economy companies in the doldrums. In 1998, Dixons, the UK electrical retailer, launched Freeserve (an Internet Service Provider), making the most of its position as one of the largest PC sellers through its PC World chain, to develop an instant customer base. Salespeople signed up buyers to a free proposition without much difficulty.

Within 18 months they floated Freeserve on the London Stock Exchange. At the offer price of £1.50 a share Freeserve was valued at a remarkable £1.51bn. Remarkable indeed, as in just over 7 months trading to May 1, 1999 it incurred a net loss of more than £1mn on revenues of less than £3mn. The public flotation valued the new company at five times the price of the parent business, a business with more than 50 years of history.

Another temptation was for companies to use the inflated value of their Internet interests to acquire bricks and mortar companies at a discount. Where they did not have the skills to manage these companies successfully, they had to recruit – or poach – new talent.

RETAINING TALENT

''Managers flee MBAs courses to join start-ups.'' If you believed the headlines, e-commerce was going to create a brand new brain drain. The concern of larger companies was that they would have to compete for whatever talent remained after masses flocked to join start-up companies, in the expectation of five or six hard years striving, before realizing the value of their stock options.

The reality was different, although, for a time, it seemed a close call. The Big 4 accountancy firms set up incubator projects as a way of giving staff a share in the profits from Internet businesses and a chance to flex their talent for entrepreneurial management. Consulting firms like Bain & McKinsey set up incubators, too, as did several large corporates – BT's Bright Star among them.

A number of Internet incubators such as CMGI, Idealab and Softbank, adopted a form of corporate venturing as a business model.

CMGI

David Wetherell, chairman of CMGI, used to manage Genesis, the rock band. In his pre-Internet days, he spent 8 years as a direct marketer as head of CMG, College Marketing Group, a specialist marketing company. His early days as an entrepreneur were less than auspicious, but he always showed the high-level energy and quick thinking typical of many entrepreneurs. He was "a little nerdy, gangly, enthusiastic – he liked to talk about ideas", according to Glenn Matthews, one of CMG's founders.

Wetherell dabbled with the idea of selling to publishers CD-ROMs containing the names and numbers of college professors. But in 1993, with the first signs of electronic publishing beginning to emerge on the World Wide Web, he persuaded CMG's board to fund a project called Booklink Technologies, aimed at exploiting the Web by selling books to college professors through their PCs and a telephone line.

To make the project fly, Wetherell hired a team of software engineers to build a Web browser. Four months into the project, Netscape launched Navigator. In short order, Microsoft and America Online came knocking on Wetherell's door. After spending $900,000 and six months on the Booklink browser, Wetherell sold it to AOL in 1994 for stock worth $30mn, which grew to $75mn.

From then on, Wetherell threw himself into the Internet. With half the proceeds from the Booklink sale, he set up @Ventures, a venture-capital unit, to take stakes in Internet start-ups, beginning with Lycos. In quick succession, he launched a host of subsidiaries to provide a key infrastructure for emerging e-commerce: Engage Technologies, to develop direct-marketing tools for the Net; ADSmart, to sell online advertising; MyWay.com, to provide customized news and information to Internet service providers; and NaviSite, to provide the technology to manage Websites for other companies. CMGI's unusual structure was designed to operate as one part traditional holding company, two parts publicly traded venture-capital fund.

At the core of Wetherell's vision was a plan to create a network of interlocking companies that worked on the Web together, each site feeding customers into the others in a virtuous, ever-growing circle. He wanted to turn CMGI into a conglomerate capable of supplying a huge array of Internet services to both consumers and corporations.

In another era, he might have been an aspiring railroad baron. But Wetherell's railroad would also have owned the stations and have supplied the picks, shovels, rails, and rolling stock to others who wanted to enter the railroad business.

His Web-based network drew customers through his portals, Lycos and AltaVista (bought from Digital Equipment) into other parts of his network, like Ancestry.com, a genealogy site for families, and the investment forum, Raging Bull. The ambition was to hold customers on the network for ever-longer periods. At its height, CMGI's portfolio consisted of 52 Internet ventures.

Like most operators, however, CMGI has found it hard to make money from the Web's massive audience. Individual parts of the network failed to see off the competition. Engage proved less successful at dominating the direct marketing niche than DoubleClick, which took the lead in market profiling.

As Wall Street's enthusiasm for cash-eating Web firms waned, the business model, built on the stock market's enormous expectations for the Internet, began to look flimsy. As long as investors kept paying high prices for shares in his companies, Wetherell had the currency to keep doing deals. But without operating profits, the funding rapidly dried up.

With hindsight, the gravity defying enthusiasm for dot.coms and B2Bs only postponed the downturn in the economic cycle, as business confidence – and consumer spending – fuelled one of the longest sustained periods of growth in economic history. Whatever the outlook for the economy as a whole, it seems a fairly safe bet that investors, in future, will be more discriminating.

What is no longer at issue is the efficiency of e-commerce, particularly in business-to-business transactions. McKinsey estimates, for example, that companies in the fashion business can achieve a 9% improvement in bottom line profitability by moving to online supply chain relationships. About half of this is from cost savings, through carrying less inventory and lower labor costs. The other half comes from increased sales, from fewer stock-outs and faster cycle times.

Companies are now more alive to value creation. The Internet boom has made widespread what insiders already knew – that investors value a business as much on how hot a management team it has and the odds on them outperforming expectations, as they do on harder assets. This has increased companies' tolerance of corporate entrepreneurs, those disruptive people with a talent for exploiting change, managing with new business models; people who can hold their nerve through unmapped terrain and are willing to stick their heads above the parapet for their pet project.

And we have changed expectations about releasing value. The IPO has become more than ever the holy grail for funding growing companies, even though trade sales outnumber IPOs as a means of realizing an investment by a factor of five. The Internet boom also speeded the development of innovative financial instruments for realizing value from spin-offs and equity carve-outs.

When Barnes & Noble took barnesandnoble.com public, they didn't just go ahead and spin off a new business unit. They issued a tracking stock, a kind of internal spin-off, which means they still own all the assets of the business being tracked, but can sell its economic value – both the risks and benefits – to investors. They also enjoy certain tax advantages from spinning off a subsidiary. Credit ratings for the tracked business benefit from remaining grounded to a less risky corporate entity. In other words, a tracked business gains some room to maneuver while also leaning on its parent for support.

AND NOW...

The fall out from the Internet boom has changed the investment picture dramatically. The initiative has swung back towards the investors, rather than the borrowers. Now it is more difficult to raise money and it takes longer. Investors – both corporate and venture capital – want to see a strong business model, a strong management team and revenue stream. They are wary of start-ups developing their own technology – unless that development is the main reason for their interest in the first place.

The amount of money venture-backed companies raised in the USA – the world's largest venture capital market – dropped by more than 60% in the 12 months following the Internet boom. Similarly, corporate VC activity was down by more than 80%, the amount available reduced by failed ventures, which reduced corporate earnings.

Corporations are still dealing with the trauma of seeing their public-market valuations – the currency they use to make investments – take such a beating. Undoubtedly, some have grown wary after watching failed ventures depress their corporate earnings.

News Corp., the media conglomerate, was one of the most prominent investors, through its e-partners venture. They backed a wide variety of new businesses, from Guild.com, who sold contemporary art online, to Ads.com, an advertising research service. However, having raised a second fund of $650mn – one of the largest funds of any corporate affiliated team – they had to return most of it to investors, who included Softbank and Morgan Stanley Dean Witter, in June 2001. The reason, according to their spokesperson, was that they recognized they had no chance of delivering the high returns they wanted in the time scales they had promised investors.

Many other media companies have also cut back their investments or withdrawn them completely. It is a good time to pick up retail dot.coms that survived the burn out. In the first quarter of 2001, John Lewis, the UK department store and supermarket chain, acquired the UK arm of buy.com, second only to market leader Amazon in the USA, for a tiny fraction of its value at the height of the boom. But, for many, the imperative for developing emerging online retail concepts has disappeared and it is a time to go back to basics.

LVMH

Bernard Arnault, the chairman of LVMH, has plenty of thorough-breds like Fendi and Dom Peringon in his stables. But there is one thing Arnault likes better than luxury – money. Having tested the waters with some minority stakes in a few choice US net firms like music site MP3.com (£60mn) and eBay auctions (£6mn) and found their billion dollar pre-floatation values to his liking, Arnault wanted more. In July 1999 he unveiled Europ@web, a £325mn fund just for Internet investment. He snapped up a stake in eLuxury – upmarket e-tailing's answer to Amazon – and purchased a 20% cut in icollector, the art and antique site. Many of his Internet investments like Zebank (the online bank) and liqui-dation.com (a B2B marketplace) were a world away from his usual taste. The initial investment came entirely from Group Arnault but his aim was to bring Europ@web to the stock market. Riding high on a wave of enthusiasm, by the millennium Europ@web had a slice of over 20 companies. Just two months later the mighty Boo.com fell taking $12mn of Arnault's with it and all Internet stock went into free fall. Europ@web's floatation was delayed then postponed indefinitely. Beginning with the sale of his stake in the ISP LibertySurf to Tiscaldi in January 2001, Arnault began extri-cating himself from the web. Nevertheless the upmarket brand man is holding on to a few select dot.coms like eLuxury and QXL auctions. Arnault is going back to what he does best so there might be life in the dot.coms yet.

Nowhere has the back-to-basics effect been more evident than in e-marketplaces, once the hottest of all e-business prospects. The promise of B2B exchanges was for more dynamic trading. With more transparency about pricing and availability, there is more opportunity for spontaneous interaction between trading partners who may not have done business together before. It is as much a new behavioral model as it is a way of doing business.

It was the independent hub operators who brought most of the inno-vation to trading exchanges. They used their industry know-how to spot the business processes that cause the greatest pain to participants and produced technological solutions to link participants' infrastructure, maximizing their distribution and buying power. They led the rush to establish a critical mass of customers and the liquidity the exchange needed to operate successfully.

But most of the independents have gone to the wall or have been snapped up. It is the big players, the industry consortia and private exchanges who are very much in the driving seat. They control a large slice of the industry's buying power. They also bring their experience of working together.

The reality today is that most e-business is conducted between trading partners who have long-standing relationships. The B2B experience, for most participants, is about fulfilling contractual obligations that have been negotiated quite conventionally. There are long-term contracts in place to govern the behavior of the parties, with set – rather than dynamic – prices.

Due to a lot of impatient money, people were led to believe that this could all be accomplished more quickly than it actually can. Innovation has taken a beating. The focus of funding has shifted dramatically in the direction of later stage, risk-averse investment. Post-Internet boom, companies' preferences for working with partners they know and trust, from the most straightforward B2B transaction to the most critical corporate venture, is stronger than ever.

TRANSLUCIS, DIAGEO'S FIRST E-BUSINESS SPIN OFF

Company: Translucis
Corporate entrepreneur: Elizabeth Paxton, Commercial Director
Previously: IT Director, United Distillers and Vintners, part of Diageo
Started: as a graduate trainee with ICL, then worked in IT for Levi-Strauss, United Independent Pictures, Columbia-Warner and IDV.

Advertisers know that 18- to 30-year-olds are notoriously difficult to reach. They're too busy working hard or playing hard to watch TV or read magazines. They go to the cinema, but only once a month, on average. You're more likely to catch them with a glass in their hand – they visit a bar or a pub twice a week on average. Once there, they are fickle in their drinking tastes, as likely to switch allegiance from Bacardi Breezer to Smirnoff Ice, from Bud to Beck's, if that's what's hot with their friends. But they have high – and highly sought after – discretionary income.

A new venture aims to solve the advertisers' quandary by reaching the eyeballs of the 18–30 crowd while they're having fun in bars and cafes. It's all in the name of winning a larger share of the twenty-somethings' spending power.

Meter-wide plasma screens hang on the walls of the bars and cafes that have signed up to the project. The screens show a continuous mix of adverts and videos of extreme sports such as hang-gliding. The package includes point-of-sale monitoring at the tills, so there is an almost instant measure of the effect on sales of advertised brands.

Translucis, the company behind the venture, is backed to the tune of more than $5mn by Diageo, the multinational drinks company formed from the merger of Guinness and Grand Metropolitan. It is the first in a series of e-business ventures that Diageo plans.

This is a "clicks and mortar" e-business venture, backed by a combination of industry know-how and the deep pockets of a market leader. Most of the management team come from Diageo and are drinks industry veterans.

Liz Paxton, Translucis' commercial director, says the plan is to install systems in bars that attract crowds of 800 or more on a busy night. The package consists of plasma screens, Internet connections and point-of-sale software. Translucis sells airtime to advertisers and broadcasts the ads and entertainment content over satellite links to the bars. Participating bar owners, who can choose what programming they want to show, take a share of the advertising revenue. According to Paxton, a three-screen package costs around £18,000 with a payback period of between 12 and 18 months. Internet access also provides the bar owner with services like previewing videos of bands and booking them for live gigs, a kind of intranet for the licensed trade.

But the key feature is the link between the screens and the tills. What really interests the advertisers, of course, is the impact their ads are having on drink sales. The main benefit of the system is that it tells them precisely how much their brand's exposure on screen is doing for sales – at which till, in which bar. It is the kind of test marketing that they could only achieve in the past by comparing the results of different ads in different TV regions.

A ready reckoner supplied as part of the package helps bar owners work out how quick a payback they'll receive from their share of the advertising revenue. So far, the licensees say the system is looking like a promising investment.

"It's a powerful tool," claims Jamie Anderson, proprietor of Café Latino in London's Soho. As soon as the screens started showing ads for Red Bull, says Anderson, "you could tell the next day – sales were up." He says his customers like the buzz of rapidly changing content on the screens.

"It's right there, in their faces. There are people jumping off mountains on bikes and people canoeing down waterfalls," he explains. Anderson says it is unlikely his customers would want to watch sports such as soccer but they enjoy the mixture of adverts and entertainment the system offers. The bottom line is that he's had a better month since it was installed and he's planning to keep the system.

As with many e-business projects, it is difficult to pin down the overall impact on takings, but the signs are that adding entertainment and interactivity to the retail experience does persuade us to part with more cash.

For Paxton, it is a chance to complete the switch from IT director to entrepreneurial business leader. So far, to her surprise, she has found that she does not feel as unprepared as she might have been.

"I hope this doesn't sound too big headed," she says, "but I've actually found it less daunting than I expected. I was thinking 'I really want to do this, really want to go into sales and marketing. But, twenty years of IT! Has it really equipped me to do it at the level I need?"' In fact, she found she could rely on many of the skills she had been using all along.

"I was literally out there on my own doing pitches to prospective customers and following it up," she says. "I thought that it would be very different from what I did as a business analyst. And actually, it isn't."

In a sense, Paxton, 44, has been storing away lessons throughout her career in preparation for her move into a more commercial role.

"Looking back," she says, "it's always been important to me to work for highly branded companies. In retrospect that's proved enormously useful. I've always been in a culture that puts the brand first. Instinctively I guess that's where my heart has always been. My understanding of marketing is probably dramatically different from the average IT director. That's what I've really been able to leverage – my twenty years of big branded companies."

Throughout her career, Paxton has always been ready to take a lead on offering a vision, for example on the future for the drinks industry. "I would talk about the way consumers would interface with the Web or WAP phones" she says, "even though I don't know an awful lot about it. I know enough to say 'here's a picture of the future – it may not be completely true but its relevant to the drinks industry, it's relevant to the consumer going out and having a wild time'."

She has also made a point of developing allies in the company. She and her opposite number in marketing at Diageo have often worked as a team, giving a lead to the business' direction.

"They'd look to me and the marketing director, equally, for a kind of picture," says Paxton. "Between the two of us we'd raise everybody's awareness of the sort of technologies that are coming down the track, and then we'd have a marketing conversation about where does our brand image fit with that?"

Finally and perhaps most importantly, she has set out to understand customer behavior. "As an IT person" explains Paxton, "even when I was addressing more mundane projects, I was considering what is the future for our consumers? How do we interface to them? For example, to understand drinking in the on-trade, you have to understand there are almost tribal groups. People think of the extreme cases, like Man U supporters, being a tribe. But actually, even on a girls' night out, people behave in tribal ways. Getting to grips with that tells you what they're going to do – and if you know that, you know how to influence them."

Looking ahead, Paxton's move has given her the confidence to consider even greater ambitions. "I'm hooked on making a big difference now," she admits. Earlier in her career, she says she valued having "a mentor, where you're in that flat bit of water behind their wake, where you use other people's stories to pull you on." Now, Paxton feels she is the one creating the wake – "Now I can actually look back and say 'I've done this before, I could do it again in a different field'."[1]

NOTE

1 Personal interview, October 2000.

The Global Dimension

This chapter puts corporate venturing in the global context:

- » think local, act global – revised;
- » venturing with the clan;
- » think judo to outwit the competition.

"Think global, act local" runs the accepted wisdom for going global. But if the thinking is done along traditional Western ideas about the way markets work, you may run into trouble in cultures that think differently. Research on clans provides a reminder about the importance of understanding those with whom you do business. It may also offer some tips for developing strong relationships as a basis for corporate venturing.

First, let's go back to basics. As they grow, companies become more complex. When the founding entrepreneur doesn't know all the faces coming into work on a Monday morning, a different way of managing is required. Without some sort of decentralization, everybody refers all the important decisions back to the founder and nothing gets done.

Inevitably communication between people becomes more formal. There's a need to codify the procedures and rules, spoken and unspoken, that all organizations run on. There's a need to diffuse them more widely as the company grows. The challenge for the entrepreneur is to provide the leadership and inspiration that keeps the original passion alive within the company and avoids a creeping bureaucracy.

There's a parallel between the corporate culture that governs the behavior of people in organizations and national cultures that give societies their individual flavor and differences. They have many features in common, like the preference for face-to-face contact or the extent to which groups share social knowledge, or keep secrets.

When it comes to a company starting to expand internationally, managers are encouraged to take account of the different cultures they will encounter. The accepted wisdom is that they should "think global, act local." The simple phrase conceals the scale of the task. Acting local actually demands a thorough insight into the habits, attitudes and beliefs of a new culture, which may be withheld, or escape an outsider.

The popular view of globalization is that this all becomes easier as global and local cultures converge. There is an inexorable movement, according to this view, towards the discipline of the market, its efficiencies and practices. This is what will shape communication and relationships between people doing business together.

The Western view of the market is exemplified by what you might imagine a bond trader on a dealing desk understands. Relationships are impersonal and probably competitive – everyone is out for themselves. There is no need for shared values and beliefs; a deal is a deal. Information is highly codified on screens or forms and widely diffused – there are few secrets in a perfect market.

However, some cultures are showing a distinct reluctance to converge in this direction, no matter how loudly their leaders may proclaim they are moving towards a market economy. They still prefer to do business with people they know. Rather than "win some, lose some," there is a belief in "win together, lose apart." These beliefs are deeply ingrained.

A stereotypical story illustrates the difference between Western and Asian ways of looking at the world. Ask a Westerner why they use a Walkman and they'll tell you it is so they can listen to their music, without being disturbed by other people. Ask an Asian and they'll tell you it is so they don't disturb fellow commuters.

Max Boisot, professor of strategic management at ESADE (Escuela de Administraciòn de Empresas) in Barcelona believes that managers of Western companies, who believe that it is simply a matter of time before emerging nations come around to their way of thinking and doing things, are in for a rude shock.

According to Boisot,[1] who ran the first MBA program in China in the 1980s, some cultures may never conform to the Western idea of the market. In fact, he believes that if cultural convergence does come about, it may well occur around the clan-like networks characteristic of Asian cultures rather than the impersonal relationships implied by the Western idea of the market. Why should a huge economy like China throw away a successful business model, he asks, when it has turned in one of the highest growth rates in the world since the 1980s?

VENTURING WITH THE CLAN

In clans, the importance of personal relationships is still paramount. Information is diffused but is limited to a favored group, since word-of-mouth is the preferred method. Goals are shared through a process of negotiation. You could stereotype interaction between people in clan culture as being closer to the ideal of the Zen master rather than the Western bond dealer.

The prevalence of a clan mentality, in a country where a company is seeking to expand would, of course, be a threat to a company that was wedded to a Western notion of the market and had forgotten what it is like to be entrepreneurial. But to the company with the skills required to take advantage of it, it is an opportunity.

So, what do clans offer? A talent for entrepreneurial behavior, for a start. Clan structures have never lost their reliance on personal relationships and a community of interest. This gives an ability to deal with uncertainty, a fundamental attribute for enterprising behavior. By comparison, many Western companies have overdone their reliance on procedures and market mechanisms. By degrees this has reduced their capacity to deal with innovation and uncertainty, and with it their appetite for entrepreneurial behavior.

Specialization – for example, as OEM (original equipment manufacture) suppliers to the computing and electronics market where their expertise in fulfilling sub-contracts to tighter and tighter time scales while meeting exacting service level standards – has been their entry card into the world business system.

And, most importantly, a particular brand of network capitalism. This is a way of co-operating that depends on connections and interpersonal trust. It explains the spectacular success of family businesses based on a clan-like structure in Hong Kong, Taiwan and throughout south-east Asia.

It is a formula for business, which has turned them into world class players in many sectors, like property, services, retailing, trading and franchising. In some, it has been enough to see off competitors with a highly successful record in Western markets.

What clans remind us about, principally, are the skills you need to build business relationships in a personal way. This is vital to a growing company's understanding of how to adapt the enterprise to an increasing range of business cultures.

But does the clan structure offer something extra to companies using corporate venturing to expand internationally?

We have seen that clans operate a kind of network capitalism, based on connections and relationships of trust. Isn't that just what the corporate venture manager looks for in a business partner? People that you can do business with – potential partners with local knowledge, skilled at operating in local markets but with the expertise to work with businesses in international markets.

Well, maybe. As long as you recognize their limitations and the effort required to establish the relationship of trust that is required of a venture partner. In short, if you are prepared to pay your dues to become a member of the clan.

Remember that this kind of network capitalism has evolved to deal with a business environment that companies in more advanced economies might see as highly volatile and disorderly. For example, information you might take for granted, as essential to doing business, is not openly available in many regions. What price to pay, who to trust, who is creditworthy – information like this is only shared within a favored group.

Joining the clan

This would not matter if you were looking for a straightforward relationship with a sub-contractor, but for genuine corporate venturing a two-way flow of information is required. The entry ticket to true collaboration may be more than sharing capital and risk on a venture project.

Do not underestimate the task of finding out what it takes to join the clan. Stereotypes, as we have seen, are seductive. But they are misleading. The answer may in fact be simple – an apparent preference for doing business with people within a favored group could simply arise from a practical difficulty, such as a lack of transport, communications and institutional infrastructure. But you might misinterpret it. Think about how difficult it is to understand humor in another language, even when you speak it fluently.

Next, consider the importance of selecting the right venture partners. It is not only the outcome of the specific project you are working on together that counts. Your partner has a hand in the husbandry of your intangible assets, like your reputation, knowledge and intellectual property. The letter of law in a contract or licensing agreement merely provides recourse if the relationship goes wrong. What is more vital is what drives day-to-day performance on agreed tasks.

Try to understand a venture partner's values and attitudes. What motivates Western firms is the need for returns for shareholders and investors' expectations for short-term results. The Chinese family business exists primarily to create family fortunes and protect them. Asian companies in general often derive a greater proportion of their capital from banks or companies within their group, and are more interested in building long-term strength.

You should note that working with venturing partners comes at a price – you have to manage the relationship with them. Technology can help up to a point, particularly as broadband networks become more widespread and the acceptability of meetings via videoconferencing increases. This promises an improvement in human contact over codified messages on screens and forms. But there is no getting away from the fact that corporate venturing is a people business.

In fact, the main bottleneck in the effort to adapt the enterprise to an increasing range of business cultures is likely to be finding enough of the people you need to manage the relationship with your corporate venture partners. Any single individual's capacity to really understand another culture is severely limited, to the extent that few of us really get to grips with our own. Recruiting people with this knowledge is tough.

If you agree with Boisot about the likelihood of cultural convergence resulting in a dominance of Asian rather than Western ways of thinking about markets, you might want to give your recruitment plans some thought. Canada has a large south-east Asian population and many second generation Canadians routinely apply their cultural and linguistic heritage, of which they are proud, in an upwardly mobile way. So do south-east Asians.

Because when it comes to developing the corporate venture network, there is no substitute for pressing the flesh. Trust and the flow of information thrive on personal contact. In that sense, the pain of going global is not so different from the pain of any other kind of growth. Keeping alive the original spirit of the company and the corporate venture both demand a continuing high level of personal commitment from the entrepreneurial management team. The jet lag comes for free.

NOTE

1 Boisot, Max (1997) ''A corporate culture in a world of global villages,''
in Sue Birley and Daniel F. Muzyka (eds), *Financial Times Mastering
Enterprise*, Financial Times, Prentice Hall, London.

The State of the Art

Hot topics in corporate venturing:

» aligning interests and proactive exit planning;
» venturing in the shadow of venture capital specialists;
» outsource to the specialists?;
» organizing for successful corporate venturing;
» deal flow – the critical factor in managing risk;
» follow the money.

"Far from being outright failures, corporate venture investments in entrepreneurial firms appear to be at least a successful as those backed by independent venture organizations."

Josh Lerner, Harvard Business School, 2000

"WHOSE CRAZY IDEA WAS THIS?"

Intel's corporate venturing program has reached a scale and importance that probably ensures it a permanent place in shareholders' hearts – and on the boardroom agenda. But the Intels of this world are the exception rather than the rule. The medium size corporate venturing program of $30–40mn quite often proves to be expendable, especially at low points in the economic cycle. It falls victim to a new management team or a company treasure, on the look out for a sizeable and highly visible target.

Will Schmidt of Advent International, the venture capital company, is a self-proclaimed evangelist for corporate venturing. But he recognizes that some remain to be convinced of its value. "Just because it's a visible $30mn program," says Schmidt,[1] "the company treasurer looks round thinking 'where can I get some cash' and spots it and says 'oh, boy. . . '." When there is a downturn, companies have the option of off-loading their investments, albeit at fire-sale rates. But Schmidt encourages investors to hang on in there.

"Corporate venturing is just as important as R&D," he asserts. "The trouble is that because it's so new, not part of the culture yet, they just kill it. They wouldn't think of killing R&D off." Schmidt believes that companies should take a longer-term view, although he recognizes that it takes an unusual chief executive to focus beyond this year's results.

"If you have no cash, then you're stuck" admits Schmidt. "But don't run round looking for someone to fire. You should think 'OK, this is an important tool for my business, right now I'm in this current situation but I probably won't be in 2 or 3 years, so how do I cope with what little I do have and manage it – because I know how important it is'."

Corporate venturing is not alone in lacking immunity from the economic cycle, of course. That would be true for venture capital returns in general. But, then, again, corporate venturing has problems all of its own, mainly of an organizational nature.

In the past, corporate venturing programs have frequently failed to meet management expectations, leading to a sense of frustration and, in some cases, cutbacks. Usefully, Josh Lerner, a professor at Harvard Graduate School of Business has separated out the cyclical issues from those that are within the power of companies to address.

The first, that you could label the "not invented here" syndrome is familiar. A new management team is quite likely to bring a corporate venturing program to a halt because it seems expendable, the pet project of their predecessors. The reason for terminating is the need to improve reported earnings at year-end. Subsidiaries possibly losing money would be bad news. Another version of this comes from the R&D department who prefer that money should not be diverted from their in-house research projects.

The next you could call "mission creep." When outside venture capital companies are hired to run a corporate fund under a contract, compensation is usually linked to the performance of the fund. They typically back the new companies or the technology that offers the highest return. But it turns out that management wanted them to invest in, say, the new technology start-ups that most benefits the firm's future plans.

Finally, it is a question of "carrot and stick." Companies find it difficult to achieve the right balance between rewarding their managers to take appropriate risks and punishing them excessively for failure. Many companies are scared to offer profit-sharing agreements that mean they have to pay out too much in the event of outrageously successful investment programs. As a result, corporate venture managers are frequently less inclined to shut down an investment in a new company when it looks unpromising than their counterparts in private venture capital companies. Writing off unsuccessful ventures looks too much like a blot on the reputation.

The issue of incentives is a bit of a minefield for corporate venturing. Managers running ventures for their companies may make millions for their employer but they are usually paid a salary just like the rest of their colleagues. The regulatory situation in most countries prevents more than very few from participating directly in the returns from a fund. This may not matter so much when the stock options are growing in value exponentially, but when they are not – as those in technology companies, in particular, have been finding – there is no disguising the lack of reward.

Contrast this with the partner in a venture capital company, say someone like John Doerr, a high profile general partner at Kleiner Perkins Caufield and Byers, the Silicon Valley venture capital specialists. Someone in Doerr's situation takes home a handsome chunk of the 20–30% of company profits retained for the partners, potentially lucrative stock options in start-up companies and the chance to cash in on them at IPO time.

The trade off for a manager could be the apparent comfort of the corporate position in the event of poor performance; the difference between a sideways move and a job search. But this does no one any good when the goal is achieving a caliber of entrepreneurial management that knocks spots off the opposition. The challenge for the company as a whole is to balance the rewards and penalties so managers take advantage of their relative security to produce a more outstanding, not more complacent, performance.

It is a tricky balance, one that requires the recognition that you won't achieve a 100% success when you invest risk capital. "Nobody wants a black mark on their career," says Schmidt, but that, inevitably, is a feature of corporate venturing.

"It's outside the normal corporate career track," he says. "You have to think how to get people involved, because you want the best people in the company involved . . . it's that thing about avoiding a black mark on your career, if things don't go all to plan – a bad deal is part of the corporate venturing experience."

ARM'S LENGTH OR CLOSE EMBRACE – THE MAIN OPTIONS

For a company with funds to invest through a corporate venturing program and an interest in making the kind of returns available from enterprising new projects, there are some basic decisions to make:

» put the money in a pooled venture fund and give control to an investment firm;
» retain control through an in-house venture program;
» outsource to a VC investment specialist.

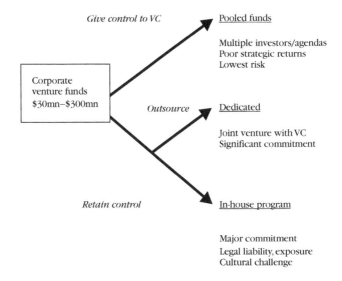

Fig. 6.1 The main options for organizing corporate venturing: invest in a fund, outsource, run an in-house program.

The choice depends on the extent to which you want to manage the venture program – at arm's length or close quarters (see Fig. 6.1).

The first option is the most "arm's length" method; you simply put part of the corporate treasure chest into a venture capital fund run by an independent specialist fund manager and wait for the returns to come back at the end of the fund's life – usually after 6–10 years. The other two options are for those who want to retain a greater sense of control over their money: you can keep an eye on an investment program managed in-house or appoint a gatekeeper to keep an eye on one managed by an outside venture capital company.

LEAVE IT TO THE EXPERTS?

In the outsourcing option, the company gains access to a flow of deals through a venture capital partner, from which to select opportunities for direct investment and early contact with possible acquisition targets.

The main cost, on top of the investment itself, is time spent evaluating projects and working with venture prospects. A key appointment is an in-house gatekeeper to sponsor the program within the company, usually with a reporting line to a supervisory group made up from R&D, Business Development and Finance. In a typical program, in which a company invests, say, $25mn over 4 years, the gatekeeper can expect to spend around half their time on gatekeeping activities and the rest on evaluating specific projects and joint venture applications.

BENEFITS OF AN OUTSOURCING APPROACH

The use of a specialist VC partner should open up access to worldwide opportunities and outside ideas; typically around 300–500 opportunities over the investment period with preliminary sifting already carried out. The fund should provide a positive return with a target internal rate of return (IRR) of 20–25%.

The VC and the corporate each bring something to the individual companies in which the corporate decided to invest. VCs typically join the start-up's board, where they provide networking support like recruiting, and they can be active in follow-on fund-raising. Investor companies can expect to provide technical support, channel access, and membership of preferred supplier programs, which helps to give the start-up credibility in the marketplace.

ALIGNING INTERESTS FOR SUCCESSFUL VENTURES

In principle, it is all so simple: entrepreneur seeks funding to develop ideas and build new business; company with venture funds wants to meet entrepreneur, with a view to transfer of intelligence and money; acquisition a possibility. However, the scope for unrealistic expectations is huge. There is a triangular relationship from the start. The mixture of goals of the parent company, the venture fund manager and the entrepreneur, is a fertile ground for conflict.

The essence of any entrepreneurial business is exploiting an opportunity in a certain time scale, usually a short one. Parent companies often give their fund managers limited freedom and flexibility to make rapid decisions – understandably. After all, they are providing the funds, taking the risks, so they need to be in control of the process. Providing adequate supervision takes time.

The incentives for fund managers are not always in line with those of the entrepreneur. If their compensation is not linked directly to the performance of their investments, they lack the incentive to match the entrepreneur's drive for success. A manager who fails to perform in a corporate fund management role often faces a switch within the company, rather than a new job-hunt. Parent companies that don't provide a safety net might not attract executives to take a turn in a venture management position. If the incentives are there, colleagues in other parts of the company can feel left out of the rewards.

Henry Chesborough, the American academic, makes a similar point about focus, but his argument is that it all comes down to incentives. In the private venture capital model, everybody is aligned behind the same incentive. If the venture is successful, the entrepreneur makes money and generates a return for the VC, whose agreement with other investors ensures that 70–80% of the gain is distributed to the limited partners by the end of the fund.

If the arrangement survives these pitfalls a strong relationship can develop between the entrepreneur and the parent company. The flow of resources – information, cash and support – from one side to the other can start producing the expected benefits. The danger of early signs of the venture working out, of course, is of too great a parental pressure to go public with an early flotation. The time scale for realizing venture capital investments tends to be longer than many other activities.

But the most common failing, the one that allows the mismatch of expectations to arise and persist, is probably a lack of clarity over the aims of the investment, on each side of the triangle. Is the aim to provide a window onto an emerging marketplace? An acquisition? Or a financial return, pure and simple? Even with clear goals, scope for the developing relationship to go wrong is large. Without them the pain of a failing or, worse, drifting investment is likely to be seen as a drain on the parent company's human and financial capital – managing the "living dead" is no job for a corporate entrepreneur.

EXIT STRATEGY

The most important decision to reach is the planned exit of a project. Managers of a growing company may resist an exit, of course, if the main prospect is a trade sale. For managers, a trade sale could mean loss of independence or autonomy, and professional investors face a big challenge in providing incentives and motivation in this situation.

The net result is a slow-moving pipeline of risk capital backed investment projects: if you took a snapshot of the total pipeline, you would see more activity at the end where new companies are coming into the pipeline than dropping off at the other end.

It is this excess which John Wall of PriceWaterhouseCoopers, calls the *investment overhang*.[2] And it is a sign, he suggests, that venture capitalists are better at investing than exiting.

Wall suggests that it would do no harm at all for investors and entrepreneurs to explicitly consider an exit strategy from the earliest stage of an investment relationship.

There may be circumstances beyond anyone's control which make it necessary to change an exit plan – the postponement of an IPO due to unfavorable market conditions is an obvious example. And exit planning is not a cure-all for every aspect of business performance. But the advantages of thinking about an exit – for example, more focused decision-making – will generally be of benefit to the day-to-day management of a company.

The most important thing about exit strategies, is to have one in the first place. The time to introduce it, says Wall, is at the earliest stages of an investment relationship, as part of the due diligence process in the case of professional investors, like venture capital companies.

The way to introduce it, if the management team is not keen to think about it, is by asking them to consider what would happen to the business in the event of the retirement or death of one of the team. Or whether they might want to buy back the investors' shares at some stage.

The overall aim is to line up the interests of the managers of the new enterprise and the investors. Or – as that is not always possible – to have some clearly stated objectives agreed for the life of the investment.

Chief among the objectives is the preferred exit route. One of the strongest arguments for planning for an IPO is that the effort it takes to promote the company for a flotation will often winkle out a trade buyer anxious to make a pre-emptive bid. This puts the shareholders in the comfortable position of being able to choose between two options: the higher return that an IPO often delivers, together with continued control of the existing management team of the company; or the speed, simplicity and lower cost of a trade sale, where there's only one customer to worry about.

Selecting the preferred exit route and defining the likely buyer for the new company gives a useful reference against which to test whether the business is heading in the right direction. Are the business strategy and structure likely to bring about the desired exit? Are the managers keen to exit or do they need to be offered incentives?

Thinking through the exit strategy often repays the effort in unanticipated ways. Wall recommends drawing up a checklist for the management team to consider each aspect of exit preparation. For example, one shareholder can hold up the disposal of a business. Keeping the shareholding structure simple from the start will avoid this situation arising.

Tracking stocks and spin-offs

There are a number of specialized routes to realize the value of a corporate venture, in addition to a regular IPO, trade sale or sale to a financial buyer. Companies can structure investment opportunities in their subsidiaries through tracking stocks, equity carve-outs or spin-offs.

Tracking stocks, also known as letter or targeted stocks, are a class of parent company stock that tracks the earnings of a division or subsidiary. They may be distributed as a dividend to shareholders in the parent company or offered at an IPO. Control of the subsidiary remains in the hands of the parent company's board. The assets of companies with tracking stocks are not physically separated from those of their corporate parents, though they do have to report earnings separately.

In carve-outs and spin-offs, the subsidiary's assets are transferred to the new company's balance sheet and management reports to new and separate boards. Equity carve-outs are an IPO of a stake in a subsidiary in which the parent usually keeps majority ownership. Spin-offs occur when the entire ownership of a subsidiary is divested as a dividend to shareholders. One of the best-known examples of a spin-off was the 1995 break-up of ITT into three businesses: diversified industrial; insurance; and hotels and gaming.

MAXIMIZING PERFORMANCE IN CORPORATE VENTURES

There is a substantial cost involved in moving capital out of a company, especially a large one, cycling it through the capital markets and attaching it to an entrepreneur. A venture capital specialist, with an established flow of investment opportunities should be able to do it cheaper and faster. So, where can the corporate venture manager gain a competitive edge?

Will Schmidt believes the answer is that the corporate venturer can structure a portfolio that allows a higher degree of risk on individual projects – with the prospect of higher returns.

"Corporate venturing raises a company's risk tolerance," says Schmidt. "It gives them an ability to take a risk on a project they might otherwise exclude, because it's part of a portfolio of businesses that they invest in." This, he says, overcomes the conventional wisdom to avoid investing in a project until it has started to prove itself, typically after 2 or 3 years, by which time the opportunity for maximizing a return has been missed.

Most venture capital companies, on the other hand, want to invest in businesses that are some way down the track; they are looking for a tested business proposition, secured intellectual property rights and a proven management team. Entrepreneurs often need seed funding to put all these in place.

What they need most from first round funders – apart from the money – is professional support in areas like commercial negotiation, intellectual property development and corporate finance. In return, the early round founders' money buys shares at a cheaper rate; at $10, say, rather than $100.

If corporate venture programs can provide the help and support the new company needs to ensure its survival as well as the funds and expertise it needs to grow, they can enter an investment confidently, while reducing the risk that usually attends investors at an early stage. To do this they have to be innovative, constructive and more nimble than their peers and competitors.

There is another edge that a corporate venture program may have over a private venture capital fund: greater flexibility over the timing of investments, both on entry and exit. Investing in venture capital funds usually has a 10-year cycle. In a private venture firm's fund, the first few years are normally spent syndicating the funds and projects. Once established, a corporate venture fund has less of a lead-time and can make investments faster. This also gives an advantage at exit – the window for an IPO can be held open longer, to fit in with market sentiment or delay in finding the right buyer, for a trade sale.

The corporate venturing industry can't afford to ignore the experience of its slightly older cousin, private venture capital.

Paul Brody and David Ehrlich identify six characteristics that are key to success in the venture capital business and analyze the challenges that they present to corporate venture managers.[3]

» Clarity of focus: it is a straightforward matter of making money for the VC investor, which encourages a clear focus, expertise in a market niche and readily measured performance. Corporate venture managers are more likely to have a wider focus, including a regard for the core business of their company.
» Flat organizations and quick decisions: important decisions that take days at a VC can take months in a corporate setting.
» Willingness to weed out the losers and support the potential winners: Brody and Ehrlich say that VCs reduce their exposure by increasing their investment in small increments. That means they can cut their losses early if the project looks doomed or, if it retains its potential, apply the management talent it needs to help it succeed.
» For corporate ventures, there are often other reasons, besides financial return, for sticking with an investment – like a strategic interest or partner relationship. When corporate venture managers miss a target, they are more likely to be able to renegotiate – providing they are not guilty of gross incompetence – and agree modified targets for the next reporting period. Their rewards for success are likely to be more modest than those of their peers in private venture capital business, but the consequence for failure are likely to be less severe too.
» Knowing when to quit: VC managers generally know their expertise is limited to start up or early stage business, not managing mature business. They realize an investment before that stage, whereas corporate

venture managers – who, after all, are more used to managing a mature business – may hang on to an investment too long.

» Reputation and contacts: good VCs are known, which can lead to first refusal on investment opportunities. They hold attractive career prospects for talented individuals. Corporate venture managers have to work hard to set up and develop a network of contacts.

DEAL FLOW

As anyone who works in venture capital will tell you, no one achieves 100% success rate on their deals. Some come quite close to it when there is adequate funding and good professional advice available. But there will inevitably be failures. A good flow of attractive deals is essential if you are to pick and choose the right projects to back.

An industry rule of thumb is that it takes around 75 leads to generate one corporate venturing deal. The first read-through can eliminate up to 90% of these, leaving up to ten prospects that may pay a visit; seven enter the final stages of decision making and attempt at gaining consensus over the fit. Negotiation, evaluation and the due diligence process can easily reduce the short-list to a single completed deal.

The key to generating deal flow is to put yourself about. Jos Peeters is founder and managing director of Capricorn Venture Partners NV, a Belgian-based venture capital advisory company that specializes in early stage funding. He was also founder and first chairman of the Belgian Venturing Association.

Peeters makes the point that the best deal prospects come from personal referrals – from shareholders, entrepreneurs, advisers and venture capitalists that owe you a favor and want to help you in return. His point is backed up by evidence from another well-known European venture capitalist, Werner Schauerte of Atlas Venture, who presented an analysis of his company's sources of business at a European Venture Capital Association meeting in 1991.

Schauerte's figures compared the number of introductions and, more importantly, the number of successful completed deals for each of his firm's main sources of business. The greatest source of deal flow was from syndicated venture capital funds; around 40% of introductions came to the firm this way. But they only produced 10% of the firm's successfully completed deals, a one-in-four conversion rate. Next came prospects brought in by merger and acquisition brokers, 35% of the firm's introductions came this way, producing 20% successfully completed deals – a 60% conversion rate.

Personal introductions accounted for 25% of the introductions and 25% of the successfully completed deals, in other words a 100% conversion rate. None of the remaining sources, accountants, and shareholders, came close to this kind of conversion rate.

Other things will help bring in the prospects. There are various methods of putting yourself about, like presentations at conference and industry events. There are technology fairs and exhibitions, although these are expensive to do well. Peeters says that his company's most successful participation in a fair was when they asked the entrepreneurs from their investee companies to man the stand and concentrated, themselves, on manning the bar.

Editorial coverage is preferable to advertising as a way of communicating key messages about your company in the press. Interviews, after all, are not only free of charge, but a much more powerful means of generating a response from entrepreneurs and their intermediaries.

But do not underestimate the unique value of your reputation – and the inescapable fact that it goes before you.

You have to work at the personal contacts if you want to generate a reliable flow of attractive deals, but what really counts most is your personal contacts. According to Peeters, this means being professional, balanced and fair. This is what gives you the credibility that persuades entrepreneurs, accountants and consultants to refer their best friends and clients to you. It is what convinces other investors to invite you in on their next good deal.

FOLLOW THE MONEY

There is a great deal of discussion about whether the main benefits of corporate venturing are strategic or financial. The best-practice test, of course, is how will it strengthen your competitive position? If the plan is to stop a competitor acquiring a promising new technology, say, then taking a controlling share in the company that is developing it, could be a smart move. If it is simply the technology that you are after, there are probably better ways to obtain it – by taking out a license, for example.

The bottom-line test says you shouldn't be investing at all, unless you're aiming to make bucket-loads of money, preferably outrageous bucket-loads. Aim for less and the chances are that that is all you will achieve. How you set expectations about performance is a separate issue: "under promise, over deliver" works well for many.

Fergal Mullen moved the aims of Cambridge Technology Partners' venture fund decisively in that direction in 1996 (see the case study in Chapter 7). Mullen and his colleagues now run a venture fund for RSA Security, the Internet security and software encryption specialist. The team also includes Barry Rosenbaum, who took over and ran the CTP fund when Mullen moved onto RSA.

"It's also a corporate fund, but it's a much bigger fund," says Mullen.[4] "RSA were cash rich and committed $100mn to the fund. We're into the market raising another $100mn trying to close the fund at $200mn." As at CTP, they are very clearly committed to maximizing financial performance.

"It's the same here," says Mullen. "In our negotiations with RSA, we stipulated that we would not be held to any strategic objectives, whatsoever – except making money." The team strongly favors the private venture capital model.

"We want to be VCs, full stop," says Mullen. "Dare I say it, VCs are a greedy bunch. But the good ones are highly experienced guys who help companies avoid the pitfalls as they scale their business and grow. They help them recruit, build the infrastructure and as they get bigger, they help them syndicate the next round of finance and prepare for the IPO. That's what a great VC is all about."

The first priority in maximizing the return is the quality of the opportunity. To find them, you need to be working in the right circles. "You don't want to outperform the VCs," says Mullen, "you want to be with them. The top priority in selecting a deal is the quality of the VC that brings it in."

Timing the investment is also crucial. It will take a typical company a series of 3 or 4 rounds of funding to go public. The "A" round gets a product to market; rounds "B" and "C" are to expand market penetration; "D," pre-IPO, is to boost the balance sheet and prepare to present to the IPO community. The RSA policy is to invest at the "B" and "C" stage.

"We're not going in really early or really late," says Mullen. "We're going in at the middle stage, the development stage." The thinking behind the policy is to attempt to match the high returns of an early stage investor, by improving the hit rate.

"The world class VCs are doing the early stage," he says. "Out of every 10 they invest in, they'll have one outstandingly successful opportunity, 2 or 3 good ones, a few mediocre and 2 or 3 write-offs. Theoretically because we're in later, we should have slightly lower returns but achieve them across more of our companies. So on average, our returns could approximate to an early stage guy."

This sets a target rate of return in the region of from high to very high. "The statistics over the last few years have been outrageous," confirms Mullen. "Some of the guys we're dealing with have been achieving IRRs in the hundreds of per cent per year. That is, they're returning 15 times to 30 times the money to their investors."

Mullen recognizes the difficulty of achieving this kind of target against the run of the economic cycle. "The market is a bit tight-fisted, at the moment," he admits. But the team is in there pitching.

"All we're doing is bringing capital, know-how and a willingness to do deals," he says, "plus a willingness to roll up our sleeves and help these VCs deliver the value they need to these companies. If we didn't treat them well, if we just took deals from them without delivering any value, they wouldn't bring us in on them for long."

LOOSENING UP

Opening the organization up to a flow of deal prospects and ventures is an important part of the corporate venturing process. The change in attitude that working with nimble and enterprising partners produces, can help shake up the more traditional business development functions within a company, like R&D and M&A.

One of the unexpected benefits of corporate venturing is the way that it can help overcome internal barriers within a company and make it more receptive to new ideas.

Enterprising organizations soak up ideas for new opportunity from everybody and everything. They don't just look for the next little improvement in a product, like next year's new features; not just the next generation of product; not just the next "big win" or "killer app."

They don't just pick up ideas for new opportunities in-house or from their suppliers or distributors. They don't just talk to their customers about their changing needs so they can anticipate what the market will demand in future.

They do all of the above and are open to opportunities of every sort from every source.

Castro's moon shot

Consider, for example, the venture agreement between SmithKline Beecham, the world's second biggest drug company and the Finlay Institute. The Havana-based research institute has produced a revolutionary new vaccine against meningitis B, one of the most widespread and vicious of childhood diseases. The prestige that Cuba's science effort will acquire if the drug is successful on a wide scale is leading commentators to label the deal "Castro's moon shot."

Under the licensing agreement, SmithKline Beecham will help finance clinical trials of the new drug, which has eradicated the disease in Cuba, to see if it is effective against strains of the disease in other parts of the world. They have rights to worldwide distribution in return for an undisclosed fee and royalty payments.

The institute's research scientists reportedly tried the vaccine out on themselves and their families to demonstrate its safety, when they developed it following a catastrophic outbreak on the island in the 1980s.

You can imagine the cultural and commercial barriers that a venture like this presents – to both parties. SKB had to negotiate with the US government prior to signing the deal to find a way around the American trade embargo with Cuba, because although SKB is a British company its vaccines business is a subsidiary of its US operations.

But apart from relieving the suffering of millions, the worldwide market for a successful vaccine against meningitis B is worth in excess of $30bn.

It may be an extreme example, but all corporate ventures open the organization to change. Enterprise thrives on change; entrepreneurs look for it and exploit the opportunities it presents.

Some kind of disruption is usually a precursor to profitable growth. Sending someone off to work on attachment to a venture partner could be the first step in changing attitudes and setting loose new mind-sets back at the ranch.

NOTES

1 Personal interview, September–October 2001.
2 Personal interview, September 2001.
3 Brody, P. and Ehrlich, D. (1998) "Can big companies become successful venture capitalists?," *The McKinsey Quarterly.*
4 Personal interviews, September 2001.

In Practice: Corporate Venturing Success Stories

This chapter provides three case studies:

» Genesis of a corporate venturing program – Cambridge Technology Partners weigh the options for corporate venturing;
» Spinning out knowledge – Parc Technologies, an academic institution brings in an entrepreneur to turn an academic spin-out into a commercial venture;
» ''Feed me'' says the pharma monster – Eisai, a research-based Japanese pharmaceutical company looks to share the risk and reward of research into Alzheimer's disease as part of its bid to go global.

GENESIS OF A CORPORATE VENTURING PROGRAM

Company Cambridge Technology Partners (now part of Novell)
Based USA and Europe
Business area Software systems implementation
Corporate venturer Fergal Mullen

In August 1996, CTP (Cambridge Technology Partners) was faced with a decision about entering into venture capital investments. Jim Sims, CTP's chief executive officer, was trying to decide whether the company should embark on corporate venturing in the first place and if so, how should deals be structured? He discussed the issue with Fergal Mullen who had joined CTP two years before as director of business development and had already completed five acquisitions ranging in size from $10mn to $120mn.

There was no shortage of suggestions. Some months before, Mullen had put together a presentation outlining different spin-off and corporate venturing models for the company. Mullen was concerned that CTP was missing out on some great opportunities of business with clients for whom CTP had developed software and now wanted CTP as a channel to market.

"We were seeing all sorts of software opportunities with tremendous companies," says Mullen. "They all wanted CTP to be the integrator of their product, because the integrator is the prime influence in the software market and if the integrator does not recommend a product, the customer won't buy it."

For example, there was JPMorgan, for whom CTP had developed a risk management solution. Now they wanted to productize it and talked to CTP about setting up a joint venture business to market it. It seemed that they all wanted CTP to invest as well and Mullen was frustrated not to be able to do so.

"We were missing some great opportunities," he says. "Like Siebel, like Clarify, like Broadview. They all wanted us to invest, pre IPO. But we had no vehicle. That was the impetus to do something. We were seeing all these great ideas and great companies. So we thought, 'maybe we should look at setting up a fund, here'."

A month earlier, a group of CTP employees had presented an innovative plan at a company conference to develop an internal corporate venture program, which they called "the Greenhouse concept".

The company had been growing rapidly on the strength of its pioneering "fixed price, fixed delivery date" approach to systems implementation – a market proposition that depends entirely on the quality of professional input. CTP invested a great deal in employee training and prided themselves on a low turnover among staff.

Sims was alert to signs of restlessness among his people and attentive to their desire for a chance to flex their entrepreneurial management skills. But he was painfully aware of the problems of this proposed new development, which he was afraid could distract focus from the core business. By 2000 CTP had a target income of over $1bn from their core business. There was no way Sims was jeopardizing that goal. A corporate venturing program required manpower, time and money. This might pull the company in too many directions at once, allowing competitors to move in for the kill. It was a difficult enough task just to keep the core business on track even if they hired more people.

Corporate venturing options

Sims was still undecided about the corporate venturing program, but under pressure from CTP's employees and managers he began closely examining the various models out there. He leaned towards the Greenhouse idea because CTP's employees had proposed it. There were other options, however. The Greenhouse concept was perfect for nurturing good ideas from CTP's employees, but how would outside entrepreneurs fit into this model?

There were a lot of fabulous opportunities out there and it would a shame to miss out. Sims knew he had to bite the bullet and make a decision one way or another soon.

CTP's analysis

Would CTP be cultivating their employees' visions or funding outside entrepreneurs? CTP had some extra cash but only a limited amount of it was available for investment.

One of Sims' major concerns was how many managers would get seconded to the corporate venturing program. It was the corporate venturer's job to find the right projects, but once that investment was made would they be obliged to closely supervise the project as well?

Just how big a part would CTP play in its investments? Should they be driving all aspects of the project or taking a back seat as a limited partner in a venture capitalist fund? Mullen had first outlined the various possibilities in detail in his October 1995 presentation and he reiterated again to Sims when they met to discuss corporate venturing in August 1996.

The first possibility Mullen discussed with Sims was starting a new ventures division within CTP. It would be closely based on private venture capitalist firms. It would be an internal division, however, organized along similar lines to, say, sales. They would cultivate employees' good ideas, products and technology – snappy projects the team came across that were not core business.

Mullen's proposed program would involve CTP and the venture division principals. The principals wouldn't have to contribute funding – that would come from CTP. The principals, the CEO and CFO of CTP, and a senior staff officer to whom the principals would report, would be the main figures on the management board. The principals would supervise all the investments and decide when and how CTP would exit from these ventures.

All the principals' decisions would be autonomous, from the choice of investment to when to dispose of it. Funds would be distributed once the proceeds had been received when the venture division sold any securities. Mullen had built in the right of first refusal on the acquisition of all portfolio companies for CTP. They would also have the right to re-purchase any of these companies at a fair market value. Instead of being a limited partnership, a new venture would be treated as a corporate division because it would be managed from the inside by a CTP team, who wouldn't reap entrepreneurial returns.

Entrepreneurs from CTP had a safety net, however; they could go back inside the company if their project didn't take off. As the parent company CTP would own about 20–50% in projects although the corporate venturers would try to keep the holdings below 50%, so that transactions didn't affect the balance sheets. Under the initial agreement, the spin-out, the initial business proposal review and the start-up investment stages out would be clearly spelt out. They should give investments about 10 years to fully mature, Mullen projected.

Creating a corporate family structure was another possibility that Mullen discussed with Sims. Employees' good ideas would be cultivated in subsidiaries in which CTP held the majority share. That way the start-ups would be kept separate. There was a real danger that pilot projects would suck up CTP's earnings like a sponge unless they were separate organizations. They might be able get round this problem by selling shares in the newly created public subsidiary first to venture capital firms and then to the public. The majority of shares would belong to CTP until the IPO. As each subsidiary went public CTP had the option of reducing its share in the business.

CTP and the subsidiaries could make savings by pooling resources such as marketing and sales. Mullen pointed out, however, that this particular model was more costly than some of the other possibilities.

Mullen and Sims also looked into issuing tracking stock for CTP. This was a new class of common stock fixed to the performance of specific company divisions or used to pick up interesting businesses. The stock would reflect the value of the new company division. While CTP held the majority of shares, the new division could obtain outside capital. It would take away much of the cost of setting up new firms and CTP would continue to be one single corporation. Investors would maintain their interest and support in CTP and not get distracted by the new projects. CTP could use its acquisitions on financial statements and consolidate its tax position.

A fourth possibility Mullen and Sims examined was that CTP would act as venture capitalists and invest in start-ups created as limited liability corporations (LLC). They would create a subsidiary to hunt down, broker and deal with the funding of new businesses. All CTP would have to do is provide the money for the investment. The equity structure would give the majority of shares – a maximum of 80% – to CTP. The rest would be divided among the new projects' management and employees. To avoid initial consolidation of start-up losses, CTP would hold under 50% of the project's common stock through the acquisition of convertible securities with no attached voting rights. CTP would absorb losses for tax purposes. Taxes and accounting charges would be minimal to CTP with this off-balance sheet structure.

The last possibility Mullen and Sims considered was that CTP could take a partnership in a venture capital fund. They could either buy a stake in a public venture capital firm or create a limited partnership for investing CTP Inc. funds. CTP could be one of the fund's limited partners and rely on knowledgeable venture capitalists to track down and negotiate deals.

By 1996 the venture capital business was mature and there were a number of knowledgeable venture capitalists around. Mullen and Sims wanted the best venture capitalists to take care of CTP's fund. But they were concerned that only venture capitalists willing to manage CTP's fund wouldn't be first rate.

Conclusion

Sims and Mullen were convinced that it was essential to have great clarity about the purpose of the fund. As Mullen says,

> "There's guys who propose to go for strategic objectives, guys who try to mix strategic objectives with financial objectives and there's a third group, that very few go for, which is purely financial. Our analysis was that you can't keep the strategic and financial aims in balance. You've either got to go for one or the other. There's no middle ground, except failure."

Finally, they decided they should stick as closely as possible to the venture capital model. "We looked at all the business models that companies were developing," says Mullen. In the end, we concluded that we should probably do it like a normal venture capital firm, to the best of our abilities." That meant they were going for the money.

"Given our position in the market, we'd probably get some strategic benefits by having some early access to some of the companies and the way they developed, based on our investment stake," says Mullen. "But that was not the primary objective. The objective was to invest some money and get a hell of a lot of money back."

The outcome

> "So we set up a $25m fund, we put around $5 to 6m of the company's money in it and raised the rest from outsiders and some of the senior execs in CTP. And it was one of the best performing funds of its vintage in the USA. Some of our big

wins were Epiphany, Interwoven, Kana Communications and Web Logic.''

After he had created the momentum for the fund, Mullen was recruited to run the European operations of another business, leaving Barry Rosenbaum to run the fund.

''He did an absolutely bang-up job,'' says Mullen. To date, out of 20 investments, there have been 13 exits, mostly IPOs, there are still five to go and only two have been written off.

''It was a small fund, mind you, but depending on how you measure it, we delivered between seven times and eleven times the investment over a three year period, and I'm very pleased to say I was an investor.''

The box below shows a timeline for CTP.

CTP – A TIMELINE

» **1991**: CTP formed from split up of CT Group; initiated by majority shareholder, venture capital management Safeguard Scientifics, Inc.
Jim Sims hired to run the consulting and software development division renamed CTP.
Adopts strategy of growth by acquisition.
» **1994**: Acquires IOS Group AB, a Swedish-based provider of information technology and software development services.
» **1995**: Fergal Mullen joins as Director of Business Development. Mullen presents options for developing business through spin-offs and corporate venturing.
» **1996**: CTP employees present Greenhouse concept, a plan to develop an internal corporate venture program.
» **1997**: CTP sets up a $25mn fund, around $5mn of the company's money, the rest from outsiders and some of the senior execs in CTP.
» **1998–2000**: Initiates investments in Epiphany, Interwoven, and Web Logic.

> » **2001**: Fund performance is one of best of its vintage in the USA.
> Out of 20 investments, there have been 13 exits, mostly IPOs.
> There are still 5 to go and only 2 have been written off.
> CTP acquired by Novell Networks.

SPINNING OUT KNOWLEDGE

An academic institution brings in an entrepreneur to turn an academic spin-out into a commercial venture.

Company Parc Technologies
Founders Imperial College, London, 1999
Business area Applications of complex combinatorial problems
Investors 3i, business angel, founders IPR

Solving problems really excites Gideon Agar. More precisely, what really excites him is solving complex problems quickly. Particularly complex problems with millions of possible outcomes. Like rescheduling 2,500 flights per week in and out of Heathrow airport so that British Airways can provide a more robust service with fewer aircraft, while at the same time observing the same constraints on curfews and turnaround times.

"We solved that one on a Pentium laptop in around 25 seconds," says Agar, "proving it was the optimal solution took another 25 hours." The headstart his team had over the rest of us for tackling this type of problem is access to 100 man-years of PhD research that Imperial College has put into developing solutions for complex combinatorial problems.

Agar is managing director of Parc Technologies, a 1999 spin-out from Imperial that has exclusive rights to exploit this hot intellectual property. The same kind of problem solving has already helped one company save $100mn a year on its "man-with-a-van" operations. Now, a group of investors including Credit Suisse First Boston, Cisco Systems, George Soros and NTT is backing the Parc team to apply it to solving network management problems for IP (Internet Protocol) networks, the backbone of the latest generation of telecommunications infrastructure. Agar and his board completed a $20mn round of funding in March 2001.

The spin-out originated from an Imperial College research operation that had begun in the early 1990s. The seed capital was the intellectual property the researchers had developed and the people that the college had trained. The aim of the spin-out, says Agar, was to reap some of the benefit of this IPR and also to demonstrate a commercial horizon to potential customers.

The research team had already gone out to win support from companies like British Airways and British Telecom, to replace state funding for university research which was drying up, but the college's mandate prevented them from operating as a commercial outfit. There was another problem, too, explains Agar.

"What was happening," he says, "was that some of our other clients weren't getting value from their research they had commissioned." Typically, a client would commission a specific project; the researchers would carry out their task and build a software kernel that provided the solution. But some were incapable of taking the software kernel and turning it into an application. That, understandably, left them disappointed and wondering what they had been spending all that money on. The answer was to focus on a narrower market area and deliver something closer to an end user product. This would, clearly, require a new approach and additional investment.

"The next phase was to start talking to the venture capitalists," says Agar. The team got 3i on board and Maurice Pinto, a business angel that had previously founded Sea Containers. It was at this stage that the investors brought Agar in to lead the new company. He was previously chief executive of a venture capital firm, had experience running a company of his own and an MBA from Harvard Business School.

His first task was to lead a review of which part of the team's research strengths to focus on in order to move closer to the market. They had also to decide whether they were a product or service company and whether they were going to sell through channels or operate on an OEM (original equipment maker) basis.

"The focus of the company is now almost exclusively IP," confirms Agar. They have a flagship product of their own, called RiskWise and they are building a product on an OEM basis for a large telecommunications vendor. The downturn in investment in telecommunications infrastructure is clearly having an adverse impact on the company's growth ambitions but Agar remains buoyant about prospects.

"Where we are now, is that we've reached the middle of the story," he says. "The end will be an exit – a public listing or an acquisition – which won't be for a while, given the state of the market." At that time, he says, there are a number of his colleagues who, "on paper, stand to become fabulously rich – as I hope do I."

So far, he says, sales revenue from two-year-old Parc Technologies is doing rather more than covering the entire $800,000 research budget of the academic research operation from which it was spun out. And as well as making money, they are succeeding in an additional aim – they are bringing in a continuing stream of work for the research team.

"It's presenting an enormously interesting network optimization challenge for the researchers to work on" confirms Agar, "really cutting edge research." And, now he adds, "there's a phenomenal commercial horizon."

The box below shows a timeline for Parc Technologies.

PARC TECHNOLOGIES – A TIMELINE

» **Early 1990s**: Signs that government funding to universities is drying up.

Imperial College decides to capitalize on intellectual property developed by research group working on complex combinatorial problems.

» **Mid 1990s**: Research team demonstrates first commercial applications to potential customers. Recognizes that to win more business has to deliver something closer to an end user product. This will require a new approach and additional investment.

» **1999**: Parc Technologies spun out with exclusive rights to exploit intellectual property. Business angel Maurice Pinto and 3i venture capital invest in Parc. Gideon Agar joins Parc to head spin-out.

> » **2000**: Parc meets first revenue milestone: funding the $800,000 research budget of research operation from which it was spun-out.
> » **March 2001**: Agar and his board complete second round of funding; CSFB, Cisco Systems, George Soros and NTT invest $20mn.
>   Parc focuses on solving network management problems for IP (Internet Protocol) networks, the backbone of the latest generation of telecommunications infrastructure.
> » **Future**: Possible public listing or acquisition.

"FEED ME" SAYS THE PHARMA MONSTER

A research-based Japanese pharmaceutical company looks to share the risk and reward of research into Alzheimer's disease as part of its bid to go global.

Company Eisai

Base Started in Japan, now in USA, Europe

Business area Big pharma

Venture partners Pfizer, small biotechs

Corporate venturing plays a huge part in the development of new drugs. Research-based innovation is not just important, it is the lifeblood of the industry. The big pharma companies engage in joint ventures with small biotech firms through licensing deals, to grab a share of their innovative skills. Small biotechs often license their marketing to bigger partners in territories where they lack presence or need extra support. In what, by any standards, is a high-risk business, sharing is essential.

"Compare it with the IT industry," suggests Jonathan Bastow, European Marketing Director of Eisai, the mid-size Japanese drugs company. "There's a small number of things that can go wrong for Bill Gates; each new release of Windows is a relatively small increment over the previous version. But in the pharmaceutical business, you have to re-invent the world every time you launch a new drug. If it goes wrong, you're back to square one, or you're bust."

The consequences are extreme. Compare the fortunes of two companies. In the same month in 2001, Novartis, the Swiss pharmaceutical giant won approval for Zometa, a drug for treating complications of cancer with sales forecast to reach $1.2bn in the USA alone; while Bayer, the German pharmaceutical and chemical company announced it is to withdraw Lipobay, the cholesterol-lowering drug because of side effects that have been linked to more than 50 deaths so far. For Bayer, this could spell the end to the independent future of its drugs division, even the company. Bastow puts the stark reality of the industry into perspective.

"Take AstraZeneca," says Bastow.[1] "They have Losec, a $6.5 billion drug. That's a huge amount of money and they're very pleased to have it. But when they lose that revenue stream, they either die off as a company, or have to re-invent themselves ... maybe it'll be AstraZenecaBayer, next time."

Managing risk

Many industries have to spend a certain percentage of turnover just to ensure survival. The average R&D spend for the pharmaceutical industry is not just 8% or 10% it can be anything up to 30%. Even that may not guarantee success, says Bastow.

"What makes this industry unusual, is that a 15% R&D spend does not ensure your success. You can up it to 25%, but you could still have a drug withdrawn once it's on the market, for all sorts of serendipitous reasons – they really can be totally unexpected."

A sudden, unexpected retreat from the market, as Bayer could learn to its cost, could mean a company losing its independence as a corporation – having to merge with someone or be bought.

The increase in joint ventures and all the merger activity in the industry over the past five years is a result of companies aiming to reduce their exposure to these high-risk situations – or as a consequence of their failure to anticipate them. It is also a way to maximize the value of the R&D budget.

As well as R&D cost reduction, the key to success is speed to market, getting to global with a few big winning drugs. The problem is that the process – from discovery in the test tube, demonstrating a clear clinical effect, showing the patient receives a clear tangible benefit from the treatment and that the effect is replicable on thousands of patients around the world – can take a long time; anything from 8 to 20 years, with an average of around 12 years.

Patent protection typically lasts for 20 years, so there is a tight window to win a payback before the drug goes generic and other manufacturers get in on the market. Also, rivals may develop an alternative compound that does a similar job, without infringing the patent, the so-called "me-too" products. For example, Zantac was a "me-too" which outperformed SmithKlineBeecham's Tagamet and became the main engine of Glaxo's spectacular growth.

That is why, according to Bastow, when companies do have a successful product, they do everything they can to extend the earnings life.

"In terms of the life cycle of a drug, you have to ramp up the sales very quickly and do everything you can to extend the patent life, because there's increasing pressure at both ends. Take Losec. It's a $6.5 billion drug, the biggest drug in the world. Every month you extend, it's worth it."

Investing in the pipeline

This is what makes the partnership deals and out-licenses arrangements so vital. The big pharma companies may be very successful financially, but they're like huge monsters that need feeding continuously. They have to come up with a billion-dollar drug every few years just to stand still. To win approvals for their products, they have to run multinational studies with a sufficient number of patients and do it quickly. For them, small biotechs are a source of pipeline products.

"The small biotech companies have the ideas, the talent, but they don't have the money," says Bastow. "It was a small Australian biotech company developed Relenza, then Glaxo bought it and boom, off it went. The public perception now is that Relenza is a Glaxo Smith Kline drug."

Most deals are signed at the pre-clinical trial stage. In a deal like that, the small biotech will receive an upfront fee, milestone payments and royalties. But they will lose the knowledge and innovation because the big pharma will acquire the intellectual property. As Bastow puts it succinctly, "If you hand over the baton, you lose your information and ideas."

Going global

Eisai is in the top ten pharmaceutical companies in Japan, but a relative newcomer to Europe and North America. Having done its own development work for a promising new treatment for Alzheimer's, Eisai partnered with Pfizer to gain approvals and pursue sales in the USA and Europe.

"It became obvious that Japanese pharmaceutical companies had to globalize or face going out of business," says Bastow. "Look at Takeda. They are number one in Japan, but they formed an alliance with Abbott in the US. We've always had a good pipeline of new developments but we needed to grow our brands globally."

Eisai is a $3bn company, of which perhaps two-thirds depends mainly on two drugs. With both of them, Eisai partnered with a top ten pharma to develop distribution in the USA and Europe, with the partners providing a lot of the selling muscle. "As time goes on," says Bastow, "more of that muscle will come from us. Our company in the USA had a $1bn turnover this year. Now there are more than a thousand Eisai people in the USA and that's been made possible by those brands."

> "Importantly, it's not been a case of 'You do the marketing and we get the check,' but 'we'll work together in the US market.' As time goes on, we'll become a stronger and stronger partner."

Bastow sees joint venturing as a growth route with lower risks than hitting the acquisition trail.

> "We knew it wouldn't work just to buy another company – you can't always afford the distractions and conflicts of a new management structure – but we realized we needed a strong partner who could fill in the geographical gaps for our major brands. Then as the brands grow it allows us to increase our infrastructure where we were weak."

The global imperative

Aricept has become the leading treatment for Alzheimer's. Eisai scientists working at Tsukuba in Japan discovered it in the 1980s and recognized its qualities for improving memory and cognitive function.

"Aricept does some amazing things," says Bastow. "To have something that actually changes the way your memory works is on a different plane in terms of pharmaceutical intervention. If you have a bug and there's a drug that kills it off, that's one thing. But this is different."

The company recognized it was on to a winner. "We brought Aricept to market in eight years," says Bastow, "which is up there with the quickest drug approvals. But it took time for the public and the medical community to recognize they had a need for it – and for Eisai to start making any kind of financial return.

"Consumers had to understand they had a problem and the health-care professionals had to be trained to diagnose the problem, before we could be reimbursed for our efforts," says Bastow. The big challenge was how to show that the patient receives a significant tangible benefit from the treatment.

"The key deficits are loss of short-term memory and attention," explains Bastow. "People forget where they put their wallet, how to sign their name, how to go to the toilet. No one had really measured these things in a controlled way. We had to work with a number of centers for psychiatry to develop a scale to measure the disease's progression … With Aricept, there's an immediate improvement in the patient and a slowing in the rate of decline due to the disease. We looked at the disease's effect on function and behavior, using the scales we had developed to measure the impact."

It is only when benefits to patients are clearly demonstrable that the health services start to be interested. When a patient is able to sign checks again or take a bus ride and return home again, there's a cost implication for nursing and social services – and for savings on other treatments.

"The most distressing thing for a spouse is the anxiety and distress of a partner who, for example, forgets the name of their grandson," says Bastow. "It can be accompanied by problems of anxiety and depression. There's a cost saving in not having to prescribe drugs that counter those other effects of the disease."

Aricept is now the leading treatment for Alzheimer's, with about 90% of the market, when a share of 30–40% is more usual for a market leader. It is also Eisai's biggest drug, by far. The company traded off a share of the profits in Aricept in favor of a strong partner, Pfizer, which could help it reduce the time it took to bring the drug to market and beat off any possible competition.

Eisai's joint venturing with big players like Pfizer and smaller, innovative biotechs is typical of middle-size pharma companies. They focus on what they are good at – in Eisai's case, the central nervous system, oncology, neurological and gastro-intestinal diseases. They aim to narrow down the task of competing globally.

''We haven't got that huge craving for a new billion dollar drug every year to keep the City happy,'' claims Bastow.

Not every year, perhaps, but the pressure is there, nevertheless. Eisai is betting that its venturing activities will lead to another Aricept and is prepared to partner with innovative biotech companies to find it.

The box below shows a timeline for Eisai.

EISAI – A TIMELINE

» **1941**: Eisai established in Japan.
» **Early 1980s**: Eisai scientists at Tsukuba in Japan discover a drug that improves memory and cognitive function. Aricept (donepezil hydrochloride) is used to treat the symptoms of dementia in people diagnosed as having mild to moderately severe Alzheimer's disease.
» **1994**: Eisai and Pfizer Inc. enter into a venture agreement for the co-promotion of Aricept in the USA, UK, Germany and France.
  Aricept brought to market in 8 years; against 8 years to 20 years industry average.
» **1995**: Eisai allocates $34mn for its R&D program focusing on central nervous system, cerebral system, cardiovascular and blood disorders; bacterial infections and viruses; and cancer.
» **2001**: Aricept becomes Eisai's biggest drug, and leading treatment for Alzheimer's – about 90% of the market (a share of 30–40% is more usual for a market leader).

NOTE

1 Personal interview, August 2001.

Key Concepts and Thinkers

This chapter provides a glossary of key concepts and looks at some of the key thinkers and writers in this developing area of corporate venturing.

KEY CONCEPTS

Corporate entrepreneur – An individual who may work in a large company, but thinks like an entrepreneur.

Deal flow – The pipeline of investment opportunities you need, in order to select projects to back; as a concept its value is that it recognizes that you'll never achieve a 100% yield so a portfolio of investments will balance your exposure.

Equity – The residual value of a company's assets, after all its outside liabilities (except those to shareholders) have been accounted for. Another way of looking at equity is as the high-risk capital committed to a business. It is risky because in the event of a company failing, equity holders only have rights to the residual income and assets of the business once all other claims have been met.

Risky ventures that may not make profits for some time need access to a decent amount of equity capital. More mature low-risk businesses need smaller amounts of equity as they can finance themselves with higher levels of debt. This has driven the trend for some cash generating companies to increase their borrowings, while returning large amounts of cash to shareholders by paying out dividends or buying in their shares.

Equity carve-outs – Equity carve-outs are an initial public offering of a stake in a subsidiary. The parent usually keeps majority ownership.

Exit – The route out of an investment, usually a trade sale or initial public offering, giving shareholders a return on their money.

Flotation – A listing on a public stock exchange; the chief way that entrepreneurs and investors capture the value of what they have created.

Initial public offering (IPO) – An IPO is a special case of flotation, for companies entering the equity market for the first time.

Internal rate of return – The average annual compound rate of return received by an investor over the life of their investment. This is a key indicator used by institutions in appraising their investments.

Intrapreneur – The term for an entrepreneur working within an organization. An alternative to corporate entrepreneur.

Investment overhang – The difference between the number of new companies entering the investment pool and the number exiting, through a flotation, trade sale or other means; a sign, some suggest, that venture capitalists are better at investing than exiting.

Leveraged buy-out – A leveraged buy-out is where a small amount of debt is used to leverage the takeover. It gained an unsavory reputation in the 1970s because of corporate raiders like James Goldsmith, and in 1984 the buyout firm Kohlberg, Kravis & Roberts financed the $25bn leveraged buy-out of RJR Nabisco with debt from the junk-bond house Drexel Burnham Lambert, the West Coast office of which was headed by the infamous Michael Milken.

Off-balance sheet investing – When companies spin off their venture activity into separate funds that have a strategic investment mandate but are not consolidated on the balance sheet, it is known as off-balance sheet investing. A corporation that spawns such a fund may have an investment in the fund's stock or may invest in one of the funds the venture company manages.

Private equity – Traditional "private equity" firms specialized in buy-outs: timing the purchase of a company that was under-performing and replacing the management team.

Risk capital – The medium and long-term funds invested in enterprises that are particularly subject to risk, like new ventures.

Spin-off – Spin-offs occur when the entire ownership of a subsidiary is divested as a dividend to shareholders.

Spin-out – A division or subsidiary of a company that becomes an independent business. Typically, private equity investors provide the necessary capital to allow the division to "spin out" on its own; the parent company may retain a minority stake.

Tracking stock – A tracking stock is a separate class of stock designed to track the performance of a specific business within a larger company. The stock can be issued to existing shareholders, or the company may opt to sell a portion of the shares to the public through an initial public offering.

A company that sets up a tracking stock still owns all the assets associated with the business being tracked, but investors can buy some of its economic interests – both the risks and benefits – in that unit. General Motors first used tracking stocks in the acquisition of the computer services company EDS in 1984.

Venture capital – This is a more precise term for the equity and loans invested in new and small companies by investors other than the proprietors of the business. Of course, neither term is unambiguous because capital invested is at risk, unless it is secured against assets.

In the UK, the term venture capital is used to include funds invested for buy-outs, unlike the USA, where it is restricted to seed or development capital for new or growing enterprises and does not include funds invested for buy-outs.

In the USA, venture capital plus funds invested in buy-outs (known as leveraged buy-outs), is sometimes known as *private equity*.

KEY THINKERS

Given the degree of interest in corporate venturing, there has been surprisingly little written about it. It is only really since the 1980s that management writers have started to take an interest and to distinguish it from private venture capital investment. The main area of interest is in the issues that the corporate venturing function can raise in the organization. Here are some key points.

Siegel, Siegel and MacMillan

Siegel, Siegel and MacMillan looked at the problem of a lack of clear rationale for a corporate venturing project. Perhaps the greatest scope for organizational problems comes from failing to make the aims of the corporate venturing program explicit. Is the main aim to make money or exploit potential for growth? There is a conflict between these aims. They point out that, if making money is the main aim, the venture fund managers should be given their head. If the aim is more strategic, too much autonomy can lead to conflict between new ventures and existing business activities.

Kenneth Rind

Rind identifies the conflicting interests of a parent company and a corporate venture offspring. His research focuses on the situation where a sponsoring firm is operating in the same market as the venture in which it invests. If the venture is successful, it may have to tailor its marketing plans so as not to conflict with those of its sponsor.

Rind also points out that there is often a time lag associated with corporate venturing that can lead to apparently poor performance. The costs of embarking on corporate ventures tend to be incurred up-front, while the returns, if any, accrue much later. A corporate venture manager may not be around to reap the credit for investment decisions made earlier. Without a forgiving and flexible performance evaluation system within a company, this is likely to lead to overly risk averse decisions.

Von Hippel

Von Hippel noted the obstacles that sponsors face in building internal support for corporate ventures within their own company. Over a given time period, according to Von Hippel, it is the ''problem child'' ventures that tend to remain within the new venture unit. The successful ventures fly, they go off to other parts of the business or are spun off as independent businesses. This is no way to win support for the new venture unit or to build a career.

Block and Ornati

Block and Ornati studied compensation policies of firms that establish corporate venturing operations. They found that firms do not compensate managers of corporate ventures any differently from other managers. The main reason for this was that companies did not want to risk upsetting managers at an equivalent level in other parts of the company by paying more. A venture capitalist told the researchers, ''The only reason for our existence is the inability of corporations to provide the financial incentives which can be achieved in an independent start-up.''

Norman Fast

Fast reported on the problems of success, finding that the success of new ventures can cause organizational conflict over competition for additional resources. Managers of established business areas within the company feel threatened by the amount of resources that a successful venture commands, with a correspondingly poorer outlook for resources for their own business area.

Henry Chesborough

Henry Chesborough's key insight is that corporate venturing has to compete in the same market as private venture capital funds if it is to become an accepted part of the management portfolio. Both are after good investment prospects and the talented people and technical expertise needed to realize a successful return. They are also, quite often, competing for exactly the same sources of investment funds. While his work recognizes that there is scope for co-operation, it squarely poses the question: should companies leave their corporate venturing investment to the experts?

Chesborough sets out to use private venture capital as a reference against which to benchmark the performance of corporate venturing. The conclusion depends on the relative performance of the two approaches. Chesborough cites the example of Exxon's experience in the 1970s to contrast the corporate versus private venture capital question in an attempt to clarify the issue.

In the mid-1970s, Exxon set itself the goal of reducing its almost total reliance on the petroleum industry. The company decided on using a corporate venturing program as part of its diversification strategy. Their plan was to make a number of external investments through participation in private venture capital funds. Then, having identified a number of opportunities this way, they would invest in some of the most promising through an internal corporate venturing program. The results provide some food for thought.

Starting in 1975, Exxon invested around $12mn in 18 firms, via the external investment program. By any standard, the investments performed very well, achieving three profitable trade sales and five successful public offerings. By 1982, those investments were worth $218mn, producing an internal rate of return of around 51% a year.

Then the company embarked on Stage 2 of the plan. They identified the most promising areas from the first stage and invested in 19 internal ventures in an attempt to commercialize them. Having focused on the most promising areas, you might expect this second stage to produce similarly impressive results. Contrary to expectations, however, the returns from the second stage were disappointing: not one of the investments achieved break even, there was not a single trade sale or public offering. Exxon brought this part of the program to a halt and wrote off their investment.

The lesson that Chesborough draws from the experience of Exxon and other companies is that there are very real difficulties in using corporate venturing as a tool to generate a company's new business separately from its current business.

There are tensions between the company's natural desire for a financial return and its strategic aims, which are generally to do with producing synergy between the corporate ventures and the current business.

Josh Lerner

Lerner's key insight is that in addition to the cyclical problems that face all venture capital investors, the managers of corporate programs face additional structural problems within the organization.

» *Mission creep*: when outside venture capital companies were hired to run a corporate fund under a contract, the compensation was usually linked to the performance of the fund. They went out and backed the new companies or the technology that offered the highest return. Management wanted them to invest in technology that most interested the firm.

» *Not invented here:* new management teams are quite likely to bring corporate venturing programs to a halt because they seem expendable, the pet projects of their predecessors. The reason for terminating might be the need to improve reported earnings at year-end and subsidiaries losing money were bad news. Another version of this comes from the R&D department who prefer that money should not be diverted from their in-house research projects.

» *Carrot and stick*: difficult to achieve the right balance between rewarding their managers to take risks successfully and punishing them excessively for failure. Many companies are scared to offer profit-sharing agreements that mean they have to pay out too much in the event of a successful investment program. As a result, corporate venture managers are frequently less inclined to shut down an investment in a new company when it looks unpromising than their counterparts in private venture capital companies. Writing off unsuccessful ventures looks too much like a blot on the reputation.

The net effect is that management expectations of corporate venturing programs are frequently not met, leading to a sense of frustration or, in some cases, a cutback in the program.

Managers running corporate ventures for their companies are usually paid a salary just like the rest of their colleagues. They may make millions for their employer, but this may not matter so much when the stock options are growing in value exponentially, but when the technology companies, in particular, are having a difficult time, there is no disguising the lack of reward.

Contrast this with the partner in a venture capital company. Someone like John Doerr, a general partner at Kleiner Perkins Caufield and Byers, the Silicon Valley venture capital specialists, takes home a handsome chunk of the 20–30% of company profits retained for the partners, potentially lucrative stock options in start-up companies and the chance to cash in on them at IPO time.

You can't pay someone in your investment group more than the chief executive. It is a problem that is hard to get around.

Rosabeth Moss Kanter

Rosabeth Moss Kanter is one of the first management thinkers to understand the role of the entrepreneur within a company. They are not necessarily the founding entrepreneurs, the people that start the business, but are to be found in every part of the organization, wherever there are people that are improving it through their efforts.

Moss Kanter says they are to be found not only in the obvious realms of an enterprise like product development or design engineering. She has found them in every function from market researchers in insurance companies to people replacing obsolete quality control systems. She calls them the quiet entrepreneurs. Just occasionally, one will hit the headlines but most of them remain unsung heroes. Like an army of ants, almost, they may not make sweeping changes or major reconstruction of the company, but collectively they are a powerful force for change.

Moss Kanter recognizes that corporate entrepreneurs are a diverse group, she says they share ways of operating in an organization which leads to innovation. They are not the classic entrepreneur stereotype so much as people who build teams and use them effectively. They thrive in organizations where ideas flow freely, where resources, support and teamwork can cross boundaries successfully. She identifies their skills as an integrative way of operating – they see problems in their wider context, make new connections both intellectually and across the company.

They find they need to use these skills to gain power within the organization in order to achieve an end result, according to Moss Kanter. They have a participatory style, achieve their projects by building coalitions and teams of loyal people. Their chosen techniques – open communication, interdependent responsibilities and frequent team efforts – keep them close to the sources of power they need to operate, access to the information, resources and support they need to get things done. The increased participation, involving staff at every level and giving them a share in the outcome of their work, can help improve an organization's performance and develop its skill base. Task forces, quality circles, problem-solving groups and shared responsibility teams are all hallmarks of the innovative company, says Moss Kanter.

Companies have to supply the information and training that encourages participation. The best results, says Moss Kanter, come from participation allied to a well-managed process: defined management structure, clearly assigned and manageable tasks, time frame, accountability and reporting relationships.

Moss Kanter says that the word "entrepreneur" was frequently used at Chipco (her invented name for a case study) to refer to the kind of person who can survive and succeed in Chipco's fast changing environment. Ideas were supposed to bubble up, with top management selecting solutions rather than issuing corporate directions. Therefore, managers at Chipco made a point of demonstrating their initiative and inventive capacities. To admit to simply improved performance in a clearly structured job would be counter cultural at Chipco, since managers were supposed to be "inventing their jobs, for themselves."

How can you tell entrepreneurial companies? They have a:

» culture of pride, with success reinforcing an attitude that success is inevitable;
» people-centered focus, a culture that makes people in the organization feel important – not just well treated, but important;

» sense that the company will turn to its people first when there is a challenge or a problem, because they are capable of handling a new situation.

The quotes of some of the employees she interviewed reflect this pride in being part of the company.

> "This is more humane than other places I've worked and it's well managed. Other places are more secretive, autocratic, with less room for entrepreneurs."
> "There's a concern for honesty and fairness, from the CEO, down."
> "It runs like a small organization – a little community with its culture and celebrations."
> "The division has a very open climate. People want to co-operate. The strength of an idea will win people over."
> "Managers will let go of employees to let them advance."

The reward system in innovative companies emphasizes investment in people and projects rather than payment for past services, for example moving people into jobs that will stretch them and giving them the resources they need to tackle the projects they have defined. In practice, this meant that managers in the most entrepreneurial companies could often see little relation between achieving a significant result and their pay rise or promotion. But the interesting thing is that it did not seem to bother them.

Moss Kanter's conclusion was that entrepreneurial companies succeed in loosening the motivational power of a conventional reward structure. People wouldn't take on an onerous task simply because there was a carrot dangling on the end of it. They would take them on because they felt honored that the organization trusted them with it, or because it was something they had always wanted to do, or because their pride in the company wouldn't let them sit back and ignore a problem any longer.

One manager, who led a team designing a new computer at Data General, characterized this quality as "like playing pinball," the reward for doing well enough to win a free game, the chance to play again.

Masayoshi Son

As well as key thinkers, some of the doers, such as David Wetherell of CMGI, Bill Gross of Idealab and Masayoshi Son of Softbank have been influential in adapting the corporate venturing model to Internet investments.

Masayoshi Son's experience, in particular, shows venturing's evolution from traditional forms of commerce. His meteoric rise to become one of the highest profile Internet entrepreneurs owes much to his skill at adapting elements of a classic organizational form, the keiretsu, to high-technology markets. Softbank Inc, his creation, dominated the emerging Internet and e-commerce markets in Japan.

Son saw the Internet and e-commerce having a transforming effect on Japanese society as a whole, not just on business. His efforts to lead Japan into the e-commerce arena face an even bigger challenge, now that the dot.com bubble has burst. The crash of technology stocks and the state of the Japanese economy mean that Softbank faces a difficult future.

Son is a third-generation Korean-Japanese, something of an outsider in the mainstream business community. His inability to obtain a bank loan because of his Korean name seems to have been a formative experience. Son went to study business in America and graduated from Berkeley in 1980. Before too long he was showing signs of the entrepreneurial talent of his role models in Silicon Valley and developed a language translator that became the Sharp Wizard.

Son returned to Japan in 1981, convinced that his future – and Japan's – lay in the digital revolution. With $1mn earned from his patent for the language translator, he set up Softbank and within 20 years turned it into the world's biggest Internet company. At its pinnacle, Softbank had a 50% share of Japan's software market, and was worth almost 10% of Japan's gross domestic product.

His investment strategy is to place hundreds of tiny bets across a range of technology companies – instead of a controlling interest in a few. His pattern has been to find hot new technology companies, fund development of their commercial applications, help take them public and then replicate them in new markets across the globe. Softbank has held shares in more than 400 companies, including Yahoo! Japan (51%) and the parent Yahoo! (20%).

Son's achievement owes a great deal to his creation of an Internet version of the traditional Japanese keiretsu, a business structure in which a company surrounds itself with an arrangement of subsidiaries, banks and suppliers, in an almost feudal manner.

The relationship between subsidiaries, which are independently managed, allows them to create synergies. Softbank-owned companies, however, have to sink or swim. Each has to contribute to the wealth of the network as a whole, and Son has shown he will not bale them out if they get into trouble. This ability to combine traditional Japanese business forms with the Internet age marked Son out as one of a new breed of Japanese entrepreneurs and earned him the nickname "e-samurai" in the 1990s.

Son has predicted that e-commerce will eventually outstrip the size of the personal computer industry and urged Japanese business to compete within the new arena. His appetite for opening up Japanese markets led him to secure a deal with Rupert Murdoch in 1996 to deliver English language satellite television channels to Japan. He has set up Softbank Emerging Markets in Silicon Valley to fund start-ups in developing countries. In 2000, he played a major role in the creation of NASDAQ, Japan.

But the uptake of e-commerce has failed to keep up with Son's dream and his investors have grown tired of waiting.

By the end of 2000, Softbank's market capitalization had fallen from a high of $190bn to $23bn. Critics claim that Son's style is too unstructured for such a huge keiretsu operation and that his companies share little in the way of focus or common agenda. Without the returns from his investments in Yahoo!, they say, Softbank would be in the red.

However, a much restructured Softbank operation could still emerge as one of the Internet survivors. Dot.com mania may be dead, but e-commerce in many sectors is still alive and kicking and growing slowly. If Son can pull this off, it would be a vindication for his vision and a testament to the ability of the corporate venturing model to adapt to rapidly changing market conditions.

Resources

This chapter provides information on:

» books and publications;
» research reports and academic institutions;
» venture capital companies and their associations.

Entrepreneurs building world-class companies and investors are faced with many difficult choices. But there is a growing range of resources available in the media, academic institutions and among venture capital organizations. We hope you find these helpful.

BOOKS AND PUBLICATIONS

Birley, S. and Muzyka, D. (eds) (1997) *Mastering Enterprise*, Financial Times/Prentice Hall, London.

Brody, P. and Ehrlich, D. (1998) "Can big companies become successful venture capitalists?," *The McKinsey Quarterly*.

Bygrave, W.D., Hay, M. and Peeters, J.B. (1999) *The Venture Capital Handbook*, Financial Times/Prentice Hall, London.

Chesborough, H. (2000) "Designing corporate ventures in the shadow of private venture capital," *California Management Review*, 42 (No. 3).

Drucker, P.F. (1985) *Innovation and Entrepreneurship*, Butterworth Heinemann, Oxford.

Frontier, Business Week's resource for small business, www.businessweek.com

Gompers, P. and Lerner, J. (1999) *The Venture Capital Cycle*, MIT Press.

Moss Kanter, R. (1983) *The Change Masters*, Thomson Publishing, London.

Pinchot, G. (1985) *Intrapreneuring*, Harper & Row.

Rind, K. (1981) "The role of venture capital in corporate development," *Strategic Management Journal*, April.

Siegel, R., Siegel, E. and MacMillan, I. (1988) "Corporate venture capitalists: Autonomy, obstacles and performance," *Journal of Business Venturing*.

The Corporate Venturing Directory and Yearbook, Asset Alternatives, Wellesley, MA.

Witty, J. (2000) "Tech's best stock play," *Bloomberg Personal Finance*, June.

Yahoo's *Small Business Information*, www.yahoo.com.

VENTURE CAPITAL COMPANIES AND ASSOCIATIONS

3I: www.3i.com/worldwide

3i is a venture capital company, which provides capital to enable growth for start-up companies, expanding businesses, buy-outs and buy-ins; sector expertise and industry contacts on a global scale.

VentureOne

VentureOne is a company which provides a comprehensive database on venture-backed companies and investors, events and publications.

National Venture Capital Association: www.nvca.org/

The National Venture Capital Association (NVCA) is a member-based trade association that represents the North American venture capital industry.

European Private Equity and Venture Capital Association (EVCA): www.evca.com/

This is an association of European venture capital specialists.

The IndUS Entrepreneurs: www.tie.org/

A not-for-profit network for entrepreneurs with membership in locations in North America and Asia, including Lahore, New Delhi and Singapore.

PriceWaterhouseCoopers MoneyTree Survey: www.pwcmoneytree.com/

Survey conducted in partnership with VentureOne, designed to take the cleanest measure of "core" investments in venture-backed companies in the USA, providing meaningful statistics on the venture industry.

Corporate Venturing Report

Corporate Venturing Directory and Yearbook 2001, Asset Alternatives, 170 Linden Street, Wellesley, MA 02482. Fax 781 304 1540; Tel. 781 304 1500.

Ten Steps to Making Corporate Venturing Work

The ten steps to making corporate venturing work:

» Prepare for the worst!
» Loosen up.
» Align interests for successful ventures.
» Structure a portfolio that allows a higher degree of risk on individual projects – with the prospect of higher returns.
» Don't ignore the experience of the private venture capital industry.
» Put yourself about, with care.
» Search for and reward sponsors.
» Keep faith with your corporate entrepreneurs.
» Consider outsourcing.
» Learn from successful business models.

"If corporate venturing is to endure beyond the next downturn in the equity markets, it must offer some structural advantages over private venture capital in its ability to manage the development and commercialization of new technologies. If these structural advantages cannot be identified, and then leveraged, company shareholders reasonably will ask why corporations don't simply return excess cash for the shareholders to invest, themselves."

Henry Chesborough[1]

1. PREPARE FOR THE WORST!

Accept that there is no single magic formula for ensuring the success of a corporate venture. Enterprise is opportunistic and depends on individuals, so each story is different.

The innovative idea is merely one part of the picture. The organizational challenge is building an enterprise culture to sustain it – one that learns to live with the disruption of innovation and with the patience to continue dedicating the proper resources in spite of false starts and dead-ends.

2. LOOSEN UP

Opening the organization up to a flow of deal prospects and ventures is an important part of the corporate venturing process. The change in attitude that working with nimble and enterprising partners produces, can help shake up the more traditional business development functions within a company, like R&D and M&A.

One of the unexpected benefits of corporate venturing, is the way that it can help overcome internal barriers within a company and make it more receptive to new ideas.

Enterprising organizations soak up ideas for new opportunity from everybody and everything. They don't just look for the next little improvement in a product, like next year's new features; not just the next generation of product; not just the next "big win" or "killer app." They don't just pick up ideas for new opportunities in-house or from their suppliers or distributors. They don't just talk to their customers about their changing needs so they can anticipate what the market will demand in future.

For example, try adopting a venture partner – or a supplier, or a customer – and spend time with them. Sending someone off to work on attachment to a venture partner could be the first step in changing attitudes and setting loose new mind-sets back at the ranch.

3. ALIGN INTERESTS FOR SUCCESSFUL VENTURES

In principle, it is all so simple: entrepreneur seeks funding to develop ideas and build new business; company with venture funds wants to meet entrepreneur, with a view to transfer of intelligence and money; acquisition a possibility.

However, the scope for unrealistic expectations is huge. There is a triangular relationship from the start. The mixture of goals, of the parent company, the venture fund manager and the entrepreneur, is a fertile ground for conflict.

In the private venture capital model, everybody is aligned behind the same incentive. If the venture is successful, the entrepreneur makes money and generates a return for the VC, whose agreement with other investors ensures that 70–80% of the gain is distributed to the limited partners by the end of the fund. Try to keep your corporate venturing activity just as streamlined.

The essence of any entrepreneurial business is exploiting an opportunity in a certain time scale, usually a short one. Parent companies have to give their fund managers the freedom and flexibility to make rapid decisions. This takes a mature attitude from the corporate, which, after all, is providing the funds and taking the risks, so they need to be in control of the process. Providing adequate supervision takes time.

4. STRUCTURE A PORTFOLIO THAT ALLOWS A HIGHER DEGREE OF RISK ON INDIVIDUAL PROJECTS – WITH THE PROSPECT OF HIGHER RETURNS

''Corporate venturing raises a company's risk tolerance,'' says Will Schmidt of Advent International, the venture capital company. ''It gives them an ability to take a risk on a project they might otherwise exclude, because it is part of a portfolio of businesses that they invest in.'' This, he says, overcomes the conventional wisdom to avoid investing in a project until it has started to prove itself, typically after 2 or 3 years, by which time the opportunity for maximizing a return has been missed.

The rewards for corporate venturers are rarely as great as for their peers in private venture capital companies. The trade off for a manager could be the apparent comfort of the corporate position in the event of poor performance; the difference between a sideways move and a job search. But this does no one any good when the goal is achieving a caliber of entrepreneurial management that knocks spots off the opposition.

The challenge for the venturing company's management is to balance the rewards and penalties so individual venture managers take advantage of their relative security to produce a more outstanding, not more complacent, performance.

5. DON'T IGNORE THE EXPERIENCE OF THE PRIVATE VENTURE CAPITAL INDUSTRY

It is a straightforward matter of making money for the VC investor. This encourages a clear focus, expertise in a market niche and readily measured performance. Corporate venture managers are more likely to have a wider focus, including a regard for the core business of their company.

Flat organizations make quick decisions; important decisions that take days at a VC can take months in a corporate setting.

VCs know how to weed out the losers and support the potential winners; they reduce their exposure by increasing their investment in small increments. That means they can cut their losses early if the project looks doomed or, if it retains its potential, apply the management talent it needs to help it succeed.

Avoid sticking with an investment, for other reasons – like a strategic interest or partner relationship. When corporate venture managers miss a target, they are more likely to be able to renegotiate – providing they are not guilty of gross incompetence – and agree modified targets for the next reporting period. Their rewards for success are likely to be more modest than those of their peers in private venture capital business, but the consequences for failure are likely to be less severe, too.

VC managers know when to quit; they generally know their expertise is limited to start up or early stage business, not managing mature business. They aim to realize an investment before that stage, whereas corporate venture managers – who, after all, are more used to managing a mature business – may hang on to an investment too long.

6. PUT YOURSELF ABOUT, WITH CARE

No one achieves a 100% success rate on their venturing deals. Some come quite close to it when there is adequate funding and good professional advice available. But there will inevitably be failures. A good flow of attractive deals is essential if you are to pick and choose the right projects to back.

You have to work at the personal contacts if you want to generate a reliable flow of attractive deals, but what really counts most is your personal contacts. This is what gives you the credibility that persuades entrepreneurs, accountants and consultants to refer their best friends and clients to you. It is what convinces other investors to invite you in on their next good deal.

Generating deal flow is hard work. An industry rule of thumb is that it takes around 75 leads to generate one corporate venturing deal. A first read-through of proposals can eliminate up to 90%, leaving up to ten prospects that may repay a visit; seven enter the final stages of decision making and attempt at gaining consensus over the fit. Negotiation, evaluation and the due diligence process can easily reduce the short-list to a single completed deal.

The best deal prospects come from personal referrals – from shareholders, entrepreneurs, advisers and venture capitalists who owe you a favor and want to help you in return. Personal introductions accounted for 25% of the introductions – and 25% of the successfully completed deals, in other words a 100% conversion rate. None of the remaining sources, accountants and shareholders, came close to this kind of conversion rate.

Other things will help bring in the prospects. There are various methods of putting yourself about, like presentations at conference and industry events. There are technology fairs and exhibitions, although these are expensive to do well.

Editorial coverage is preferable to advertising as a way of communicating key messages about your company in the press. Interviews, after all, are not only free of charge, but a much more powerful means of generating a response from entrepreneurs and their intermediaries.

But do not underestimate the unique value of your reputation – and the inescapable fact that it goes before you.

7. FIND SPONSORS AND KEEP THEM HAPPY

Ask successful corporate venturers who or what helped them through their darkest hour with a project, and they'll probably mention someone's name. Take note and you are on the way to identifying an invaluable resource: the in-house sponsor. Usually, a handful of a company's managers are doing the lion's share of the successful sponsoring. The rest get in the way or lack the business judgment essential to the task.

Sponsors are the critical link between top management and a company's entrepreneurial managers. They question, guide and cajole them and generally make them more house-trained.

It is sometimes an uncomfortably exposed role, but courageous sponsors who understand and care about the project and its entrepreneurial team are indispensable to corporate venturing success. They are rare and generally under-appreciated. Treasure and reward them.

8. KEEP THE FAITH

If you believe in your corporate ventures, you must be prepared to overcome corporate resistance and support your venture managers. If you lose confidence in a project, let the venture manager be the first to know. Make sure to reward them if they succeed. Support them if they fail in a good and honest attempt. You won't attract people of the caliber you want to the role if they have doubts about their career prospects.

Organizational inertia and resistance tends to break up corporate venture teams and move members to other projects. Obviously, members will move in and out as the demand for their talents changes, but a core team with the collective knowledge of lessons learned is key to a pattern of success. There is an investment in innovative ideas and entrepreneurial endeavor - cut your losses, but don't bury the experience with the body.

9. CONSIDER OUTSOURCING

In the outsourcing option, the company gains access to a flow of deals through a venture capital partner, from which to select opportunities for direct investment and early contact with possible acquisition targets.

The use of a specialist VC partner should open up access to worldwide opportunities and outside ideas; typically around 300–500 opportunities over the investment period with preliminary sifting already carried out. The fund should provide a positive return with a target IRR (internal rate of return) of 20–25%.

The main cost, on top of the investment itself, is time spent evaluating projects and working with venture prospects. A key appointment is an in-house gatekeeper to sponsor the program within the company, usually with a reporting line to a supervisory group made up from R&D, Business Development and Finance. In a typical program, in which a company invests, say, $25mn over 4 years, the gatekeeper can expect to spend around half their time on gatekeeping activities and the rest on evaluating specific projects and joint venture applications.

10. LEARN FROM SUCCESSFUL BUSINESS MODELS

There are companies that have screwed up badly in corporate venturing. Learning from them isn't easy, as no one likes a failure. But there are also success stories (see the case studies) and examples that seem to offer some generic insights.

CREATING VALUE FROM TALENT

One company that shows every sign of having developed a sustainable model for corporate venturing is Cambridge Consultants. CCL's site at Cambridge's Science Park exudes an impressive air of hands-on talent. Enthusiastic engineers bring prototypes to market at a brisk pace. Bright managers keep a close eye on the bottom-line. They are starting to build closer relations with the local research and business community.

Parent company Arthur D. Little is looking for a more entrepreneurial approach. They want them to retain more value from their clever ideas and products, by incubating new companies and spinning them off.

Crucially, CCL has found a way to capitalize on their expertise while holding on to a share of the high value intellectual copyright – instead of, say, selling it to whichever client commissioned them to develop a new product. This is a valuable business model.

"We're good at doing clever things, quickly" is how managing director Howard Biddle describes it. The company's main strength is in applying innovative technology to high volume consumer markets, from packaging and printing to WAP videophones. Biddle says the spin-off approach is beginning to make some serious money.

"The companies we've spun off now have a combined turnover of around £200mn," he says. "If we hadn't done the spin-outs for Inca Digital and Cambridge Silicon Radio, the same people working for us would have generated around £15mn of contribution over five years. However the companies we've created we expect to be worth more than £1bn, in terms of market capitalization."

In 2000, Clare Ruskin, the company's product development director, completed the first round funding for CCL's latest spin-off, Cyan Technology.

"Cyan is a company designed to market a new low power micro-controller for products like mobile phones, pagers and gas meters," says Ruskin. CCL's engineers have taken out the core micro-controller technology they developed for a number of different applications and modularized it.

"We've already used the technology in a dozen or more of our own products," says Ruskin, "and now were trying to exploit it by forming a separate company to do stand-alone micro-controllers. There'll be a family of standard components that people can buy for their applications." The business process, itself, is also something of an innovation.

"We're doing the spin-off without losing any CCL people," says Ruskin. "We've recruited David Griffiths, an entrepreneur, to take the technology out and licensed the technology to the new company." CCL holds onto the intellectual property in the technology and keeps a large stake in the new company. The whole process, Ruskin says, took around six months and the company is already looking for its next spin-off.

Having completed this one, Ruskin is feeling a great sense of relief. She says the key to doing it all efficiently is to sort out the business arrangements with each partner in the process, before entering into lengthy legal negotiations.

She is skeptical about projects that don't have sound technological and business foundations. "You can't do all the dot.com things that are based on a night in the pub," she says. "It's got to be based on something that can go forward and create real value." She doubts that government initiatives will achieve a great deal.

"I'm not sure there's much the government can honestly do," says Ruskin. "It's more a case of encouraging the core engineering companies that we have in this country to be bold and creative."

Can CCL keep their talented staff busy and motivated while holding onto their clients and generating the spin-offs? Biddle has the answer.

"If you're going to start new companies," he points out, "then people are going to leave. But, frankly, thinking long term, that's going to attract good people. Because we've got a soft incubator environment where people can come to learn their engineering skills and then move into their own businesses while, if you like, being sponsored by CCL. We're going to get some good people applying."[2]

NOTES

1 Chesborough, H. (2000) "Designing corporate ventures in the shadow of private venture capital," *California Management Review*, Vol. 42, No. 3.

2 Personal interviews, October 2000.

Frequently Asked Questions (FAQs)

Q1: Why do corporate venturing?

A: At the most basic level corporate venturing takes a good idea and makes it into money. It is a way of managing risk and cutting back on the research and development budget, while speeding up the process of getting products to market.

Pharmaceutical and technology companies are prime exponents of corporate venturing. See examples: Chapter 6, "Castro's moon shot"; Chapter 7, Eisai case study; Chapter 2, Iona Software and Chapter 7, Cambridge Technology Partners and Parc Technologies.

Q2: What are the main options for a corporate venturing program and how do you maximize performance?

A: You can set up an in-house program, outsource to a venture capitalist firm, or put your money in a pooled venture fund. See Chapter 3, "Types of corporate venturing programs" and Chapter 6 "Arms' length or close embrace – the main options".

To see how one company examined the main options, see the case study on Cambridge Technology Partners in Chapter 7.

There are plenty of tips on choosing the right investment, but remember no venture is foolproof. See Chapter 6, "Maximizing performance in corporate ventures" and "Follow the money."

Q3: What is the relationship between venture capital and corporate venturing?

A: Corporate venturing has generally had to follow venture capitalists' lead, without achieving the same spectacular results. However current research proves returns from corporate venturing can be just as successful as from private venture capital – especially when there is a strategic overlap of interests between the parent company and the investment. See Chapter 3.

Q4: How has the Internet affected corporate venturing?

A: We've all heard about the corporations that got burned when the dot.com bubble burst. Many companies are still dealing with the trauma of seeing their public-market valuations – the currency they use to make investments – take a beating. It's back to basics for most of them. See Chapter 3 timeline and Chapter 4.

Q5: What influence does globalization have on corporate venturing?

A: There is more to globalization than simply dressing up Western practices with a veneer of another culture. Despite what their leaders say about moving towards a market economy, many cultures are still reluctant to do business with outsiders. Because it is very much a people business, corporate venturing relies on personal contact and the trust that allows the flow of information – a kind of clan mentality. But you have to pay the admission price before you join the clan – see Chapter 5.

Q6: Where do the best investment prospects come from?

A: The best source is personal introduction from shareholders, entrepreneurs, advisers and venture capitalists who want to bring you in on a deal. You can develop personal contacts at conferences and industry events, but remember your reputation goes before you. See Chapter 6,

"Deal Flow." The Iona mini case in Chapter 2 shows just how new businesses sometimes get together in corporate ventures.

Q7: What makes an exit strategy so important?

A: It might sound a bit obvious but you can't realize the value of a corporate venture until you exit. Planning the exit from the start helps align the interest of entrepreneur and investor and increases the chances of maximizing a return on investment. Three main ways of obtaining your money are IPOs, trade sales and sales to financial buyers. See Chapter 2, "Corporate venturing programs" and Chapter 6, "Exit strategy."

Q8: Are corporate venturers rewarded as well as their private venture capitalist counterparts?

A: This is a thorny issue especially when a company is trying to motivate and retain the best employees. The honest answer is no, but corporate venture fund managers also pay a smaller price for failures. See Chapter 6, "Whose crazy idea was this?" and "Aligning interests for successful ventures."

Q9: If corporate venturing brings rewards, why are corporate venturing programs frequently scrapped?

A: It is an obvious target for the company accountants trying to balance the books, especially during an economic downturn. New management teams have different investment strategies to their predecessors. See Chapter 6, "Whose crazy idea was this?". Success brings its own problems – see Norman Fast's work, reported in Chapter 8.

Q10: What can corporate venturers offer new businesses, besides funding?

A: Experience, management skills and, if they know their stuff, a readiness to make investments at an earlier stage than VCs, in return for higher returns. See the theory in Chapter 2 and the practice: "Translucis, Diageo's first e-business spin off" in Chapter 4 and the three case studies in Chapter 7.

Index

Printed and bound in the UK by
CPI Antony Rowe, Eastbourne

Printed and bound by CPI Group (UK) Ltd, Croydon, CR0 4YY

13/04/2025

14656559-0001